M000220100

# LEADING CREATIVE TEAMS

## MANAGEMENT CAREER PATHS FOR DESIGNERS, DEVELOPERS, AND COPYWRITERS

*Eleazar Hernández*

**Apress®**

*Leading Creative Teams: Management Career Paths for Designers, Developers, and Copywriters*

Eleazar Hernández
San Antonio, Texas, USA

ISBN-13 (pbk): 978-1-4842-2055-9      ISBN-13 (electronic): 978-1-4842-2056-6
DOI 10.1007/978-1-4842-2056-6

Library of Congress Control Number: 2016956457

Managing Director: Welmoed Spahr
Acquisitions Editor: Robert Hutchinson
Developmental Editor: Linda Laflamme
Editorial Board: Steve Anglin, Pramila Balen, Laura Berendson, Aaron Black, Louise Corrigan,
    Jonathan Gennick, Robert Hutchinson, Celestin Suresh John, Nikhil Karkal,
    James Markham, Susan McDermott, Matthew Moodie, Natalie Pao, Gwenan Spearing
Coordinating Editor: Rita Fernando
Copy Editor: Brendan Frost
Compositor: SPi Global
Indexer: SPi Global

Distributed to the book trade worldwide by Springer Science+Business Media New York, 233 Spring Street, 6th Floor, New York, NY 10013. Phone 1-800-SPRINGER, fax (201) 348-4505, e-mail orders-ny@springer-sbm.com, or visit www.springeronline.com. Apress Media, LLC is a California LLC and the sole member (owner) is Springer Science + Business Media Finance Inc (SSBM Finance Inc). SSBM Finance Inc is a Delaware corporation.

For information on translations, please e-mail rights@apress.com, or visit www.apress.com.

Apress and friends of ED books may be purchased in bulk for academic, corporate, or promotional use. eBook versions and licenses are also available for most titles. For more information, reference our Special Bulk Sales–eBook Licensing web page at www.apress.com/bulk-sales.

Any source code or other supplementary materials referenced by the author in this text is available to readers at www.apress.com. For detailed information about how to locate your book's source code, go to www.apress.com/source-code/.

Printed on acid-free paper

## Apress Business: The Unbiased Source of Business Information

Apress business books provide essential information and practical advice, each written for practitioners by recognized experts. Busy managers and professionals in all areas of the business world—and at all levels of technical sophistication—look to our books for the actionable ideas and tools they need to solve problems, update and enhance their professional skills, make their work lives easier, and capitalize on opportunity.

Whatever the topic on the business spectrum—entrepreneurship, finance, sales, marketing, management, regulation, information technology, among others—Apress has been praised for providing the objective information and unbiased advice you need to excel in your daily work life. Our authors have no axes to grind; they understand they have one job only—to deliver up-to-date, accurate information simply, concisely, and with deep insight that addresses the real needs of our readers.

It is increasingly hard to find information—whether in the news media, on the Internet, and now all too often in books—that is even-handed and has your best interests at heart. We therefore hope that you enjoy this book, which has been carefully crafted to meet our standards of quality and unbiased coverage.

We are always interested in your feedback or ideas for new titles. Perhaps you'd even like to write a book yourself. Whatever the case, reach out to us at editorial@apress.com and an editor will respond swiftly. Incidentally, at the back of this book, you will find a list of useful related titles. Please visit us at www.apress.com to sign up for newsletters and discounts on future purchases.

*The Apress Business Team*

*To Kathy...*

*Who gave me the freedom to explore my creative ideas and the support to act on them.*

# Contents

# About the Author

**Eleazar Hernández** is the owner and Creative Director of Hernández Design Company (*hernandez-design.com*). He has specialized in award-winning branding, identity, product, packaging, retail, and web designs for national and international clients. Over the past 20 years he has produced breakthrough brand design strategies for clients such as Anne Klein, Steven Kretchmer, New York State Museum, Planned Parenthood, Kaiser Family Foundation, Univision, the Dallas Cowboys, and Vivente Tasty Foods Mexico. Hernández has received numerous awards from many major design and advertising publications in the United States and Europe and was named one of the Designers to Watch by *Graphic Design: USA* magazine. He has lectured extensively to student and professional groups on the business side of design and his own creative process. He has also judged numerous design and advertising competitions on the local, regional, and national levels.

# Acknowledgments

Thanks go to the friends and associates who I have worked with over the years that helped provide the inspiration and experience that led to this book. Teammates and leaders that I worked alongside while enlisted in the US Air Force, in particular, James Person, Mark Bennett, Armando Espino, Kenneth Horton, and Franklin Wheeler, Jr. My design professor and mentor Louis Ocepek. My creative, advertising, and marketing friends and associates Tara Ricard, Paul Knapick, Katie Diduch, Andrew Anguiano, Kazim Fahim, Olga Garces, Mary Carmen Ruiz-Sesssions, Charles Davis, Jennifer Katz, Christopher Pawlik, Steve Young, Dora Guiterrez, Kay Rangel, Ramon Hernandez, Kristina Leh, Jona Haga-Camacho, Jimmy Nichols, Alex Alvarado, Paul Lazo, Rick Holcomb, Nathan Post, Chad Wooten, Frank Guerra, Beth Wammack, Carey Quackenbush, Victor Noriega, Barbie Rugen and Tita Sartorio.

Big thanks go to friends and associates whom I interviewed for the book or who provided graphics, including Claudia Camargo, Colin Harman, Elizabeth Grace Saunders, Kevin Lane, Kim Arispe, Lisette Sacks, Monica Ramirez Nadela, Todd Henry, Jessica Walsh, and Debbie Millman.

Thanks to everyone at Apress, most notably Robert Hutchinson, who helped me get this project off the ground by graciously responding to my initial (and somewhat rambling) e-mail. Thanks to Rita Fernando for being my guide and gently keeping me on track throughout the process. Thanks also goes to Linda Laflamme for editing the book and providing humorous and insightful recommendations that helped ease me into the world of publishing.

A big thanks goes to my parents, Mildred and Eleazar, who while they may still be a little unsure of what it is I actually *do* for a living, are nonetheless proud. Yes, Mom and Pop, I can make a great living from drawing stuff!

Thanks to my kids and their spouses, Ryan, Ashley, Adam, Kate, Joanna, and April. Shout-outs to my grandbabies (I know, I look surprisingly young to have grandbabies) Eloise, Gwyneth, Oliver, Max and Violette—your Poppy loves all of you!

Finally, a sincere and heartfelt thanks to my amazing wife Kathy. She has supported every crazy career idea I've had, from wanting to be a doctor or an architect, to a professional wrestler (yes, a WWE pro wrestler), an art historian, or a Preclassic Maya archaeologist. Through it all, she has always been my source of support and guidance. My partner in crime, the Wonder Woman to my Batman, the peanut butter to my jelly, the straw in my soda... my girl. I love you. Thank you.

# Introduction

Working your way through the ranks to creative director is a goal of many creative men and women in the design, advertising, interactive, or other creative industries. In my experience I have found that there are typically two paths taken by those who make it to creative director: straightforward or circuitous.

Those who have made it via a straightforward career path have gone from one rank to the next over a series of years with relative ease. These creatives appear to have been born with a silver pencil in their mouths. They seem to have the Midas touch for finding and developing great ideas. They have a knack for finding the smallest nugget of insight in brainstorm sessions and can develop it into a full-blown successful campaign. They seem to have it all.

Creatives who have made it to creative director via a more circuitous route take hits here and there. Their career paths resemble a rollercoaster ride of high and low points until they finally reach creative director. They may have jumped to different agencies for promotions or taken risks joining an agency with a bad reputation only to depart quickly upon learning the agency's negative reputation was well-deserved. They may have tried to work with an in-house creative team, only to find it less than satisfying and somewhat rote. They could have gone out on their own with dreams of grandeur, but succumbed to taking any client that walked through the door in order to remain afloat and pay their bills. These creative directors are just as talented and capable as those on the straightforward path; they are simply a little more adventurous and willing to take more risks.

Is it always one path or the other? No. It could be a combination of the two. In fact, the majority of the creative directors I know tend to fall somewhere in between. Regardless of which route you happen to take, I'm not going to try to make you believe that it's going to be easy. It will be hard work. You must be driven. Driven to succeed. Driven to lead. Driven to produce the best, most insightful, engaging creative possible—at all times. There are no free passes when you're a creative leader.

Unfortunately, there is no magic bullet that is going to help you all the way. You can't just read a book and believe that you can follow every piece of information to get what you want. I can point you in the right direction, but not draw a detailed road map. Why? Because you will encounter specific nuances in every job that will be unique to you—your temperament, your creativity, your experience, your personality, and your skills.

# Learn from Everything

My personal journey has been exciting and frustrating, fulfilling and disheartening, exhilarating and infuriating. It has been 20 years of a constant duality. On one hand I have met great people who have taught me about creativity, leadership, supervision, presentations, team interactions, and much more. They have helped me grow and improve. On the other hand, I have also met and worked with huge assholes who have taught me how not to lead, how not to critique, how not to interact with people, how not to gain trust, or how not to share the credit. Whether experiences have been positive or negative, I learned from every encounter, every situation, every success, and even every failure.

To be a successful creative director, you must be a student of the industry, a student of life. When you look out into the world, what do you see? Do you really look? Successful creative directors are students of life. They are impacted, influenced, or inspired by virtually everything. The best creative directors also know how to inspire this kind of behavior in others.

# Be a Great Leader

To be a great creative director you must also be a great leader, not only of your creative team, but of the agency as a whole. This isn't something that comes naturally to many people, and is in fact one of the biggest deficits I have found in some creative leaders. One of the benefits of my time in the military is that I was required to take leadership and supervision classes as I progressed up the career ladder. There isn't anything like that for creatives who are being promoted into positions of leadership. I wish there were.

There are how-to manuals for designing websites, collateral material, posters, or ads. There are lots of books with multiple subjects regarding the creative process, or retrospectives of work produced by creative directors and their teams, but there isn't anything out there that actually helps creatives prepare to move into leadership.

When creative professionals move up the ladder they are expected to take up the additional responsibilities of leadership while maintaining the skills that led them to the promotion. However, the truth is that just because someone is a good art director, doesn't mean they will be a good senior art director. Likewise, a good associate creative director won't necessarily make a good creative director. There are skills that must be developed and understood to be able to move up the ranks successfully, but sadly there aren't any companies (that I know of) that actually provide training to people moving up the career ladder. That's where this book comes in.

# The Story Behind My Story

For years, I have talked about wanting to write a book about the information I believe creatives should have if they want to make it to creative director. I finally put my money where my mouth was. In late 2015, I was asked to give a talk to AIGA's San Antonio chapter. They asked me to speak about anything I felt passionate about. I decided to speak about being a creative director, or more specifically, how not to suck as a creative director.

In that presentation, I gave tips along with examples that explained how to effectively lead a creative team. The audience was engaged and asked some very good questions. (Thanks AIGA SA!) Following my talk, I told my wife Kathy that I thought I would pitch what I presented as a book idea. She agreed. One thing led to another, and before I knew it, I was writing the book you now hold in your hands.

If you are currently in school, or if you have already graduated and are work-ing, you know that leadership and supervision skills for creatives is not some-thing required as part of your creative curriculum. As creative people, we are taught the basics of design or writing. We are challenged to solve the creative aspects associated with our future clients' marketing challenges. Most of our leadership and supervisory skills come from the experiences we have in the work force. Too succeed in the indistry, you must be able to lead. This book will provide you with tips and insights you can use.

# Coming Attractions

*Leading Creative Teams* is the result of my desire to help out hungry creatives (designers, art directors, copywriters, developers, etc.) who want to move up the ranks and prepare for leadership. While I do not profess to have answered all questions associated with leadership, I do believe that anyone with the desire to lead will find a solid foundation of information. My goal in this book is to expose you to the various aspects of leadership that many creatives either don't think about or take for granted, aspects that are of key importance if you want to evolve into a good creative leader. I hope this book provides you with useful guidelines on how to think through facets of leadership and how you should prepare for them. Here's a breakdown of what's covered where:

- **Chapter 1** defines creative leadership, works through the basics, and provides tips on preparing to lead a team of creative professionals.

- **Chapter 2** delves a little deeper into what you should be prepared to do as a creative leader along with some of the personalities you'll have on your teams.

- **Chapters 3** and **4** get a little more specific into leading creative teams in the advertising and design industries. Although they share similarities, there are slight differences in terms of specific knowledge when it comes to the elements and principles of graphic design.

- **Chapter 5** goes over brainstorming, which is a place where most creative directors separate themselves from the pack. I also provide several exercises that can help you brainstorm with your teams.

- **Chapter 6** introduces the idea of sketching and thumbnailing, something that I strongly believe is a key skill that all creatives should have. As a leader, you should be able to quickly get your ideas out and relay them to your team with minimal loss of meaning. You don't have to be Michelangelo, but you should be able to develop a shorthand that relays information to your team quickly and accurately.

- **Chapter 7** provides tips on critiquing your team's work. Being able to provide honest and constructive feedback will help you inspire your team to produce their best work.

- **Chapter 8** goes over the pitch and provides a model for pitching your work. Being able to pitch is an invaluable skill for creative directors because it will help you gain clients or obtain approval for your team's work. It can mean the difference between having and keeping a job or not.

- **Chapter 9** gets a little tactical with copywriting. This is a skill that you must have. You don't have to be an expert copywriter, but you should be able to guide and critique your team's work.

- **Chapter 10** provides a little more tactical information on producing a TV and radio spot. Excelling at creating a 30-second spot for broadcast is vital for creative directors, but the necessary skills are not typically taught in degree programs for creatives.

- **Chapter 11** provides insight into working your way up to the position of creative director. It answers questions on education, experience, and management.

- **Chapter 12** reminds you about the importance of your greatest asset: your creative team. You'll learn why investing in your people is important, as well as ideas for keeping them engaged and motivated.

- **Chapter 13** rounds out the book with interviews from several of my friends and colleagues who are leading their own creative teams. As you read through these pages, you will notice that the majority of the leaders interviewed are women—despite the fact that women make up only 3% of creative directors in our industry. I am honored to support the movement to decrease the disparity among creative leaders, and I feel very fortunate to have several highly creative female leaders in this book to provide insight for you.

As you work through the chapters, think about how you can integrate some of the ideas into your workplace. Will they work? If they won't, how can you adjust them to make them your own? In the end you will customize your own leadership experience. Ready? Let's roll.

# Start with a Blank Piece of Paper

## In the beginning…

What is it that takes a person from the beginning of their creative career to reaching the highest levels of creative leadership? Some people just seem to excel at leadership and strategy while others never seem to quite get it. We hear stories of creative directors (CDs) who are brilliant, but have explosive tempers. These are the leaders that fly off the handle when something doesn't go as planned. There are other creative leaders that seem to be happy doing mediocre work for mediocre clients. They never strive for anything better. They never really seem to have the passion you'd expect from a creative leader. Then there are those rare few. Those creative leaders who seem to have it all: a brilliant creative mind, an eye for spotting talent, and the charisma to lead a team through good times and bad. This is the person creatives want to follow, and for whom they will do their best work. This is the kind of creative leader that gets the best out of everyone they come into contact with.

© Eleazar Hernández 2017

E. Hernández, *Leading Creative Teams*, DOI 10.1007/978-1-4842-2056-6_1

Underneath all of that, a great creative leader must have passion and drive. A *passion* for new ideas and the relentless *drive* to make them real. Whether you are a copywriter or an art director, you will have to develop a specific set of skills to help you along your particular career path, but there are specific skills that leaders possess that typically propel them head and shoulders above the rest.

Let's not beat around the bush: CDs need great taste and excellent judgment. More than just making the work look good, they must also have a sense of what it takes to connect with the audience. They need to know how far to push an idea while remaining relevant. A great CD can add to his team's ideas to move them from good to great.

Let's jump right in to what this book will lead you to—the skills needed to be a great creative leader.

# Where Creatives Are Lacking

There is a basic fault with career progression in the creative industry. *Training.* There is not any training that provides junior and midlevel creatives with the skills needed to successfully progress in their careers. Many times, as creatives increase their proficiency within their chosen specialty (graphic design, copywriting, art direction, photography, etc.) they are given a promotion and immediately expected to take on more responsibilities. Those responsibilities could include supervising personnel, determining budgets, presenting ideas to internal staff and external clients, and hiring or even firing people.

There are times when creatives handle the promotion well and are able to take on the additional responsibilities. They may hit a few bumps in the road, but they learn quickly and become proficient at their new job. They will survive. Many times, however, recently promoted creative leads go through a trial-by-fire only to come up short at the expense of their coworkers, their company, their clients, or even their job. This problem became very apparent to me as I progressed through the ranks. Working with and for creatives at various levels, I was able to view firsthand the differences between creatives who could lead and those who could not.

As a CD, you will need to get the best out of the people around you whether they are art directors, account executives, media planners, public relations, photographers, printers, or directors. As the creative lead, it's your job to have the vision and sell that to everyone—not just the client, but their creative and account team. You need to get everyone onboard so you can all move toward the same goal.

Working hard and always trying to do your best work was what helped get you the gig. It wasn't easy. You've busted your ass always trying to knock out great work. You've stayed late to ensure that your projects are delivered on time. You've consistently demonstrated to those around you that you are a great creative. Now you've made it! You landed the promotion you wanted. You got the raise. You got the title. Now you just have to keep the job.

# Good Fortune

I believe that everyone's frame of reference informs what kind of creative leader they are. If you worked for a micromanaging tyrant, there is a chance you may manage the same way. If you were supervised by someone who is very hands-off and gave you room to move, you may acquire some of those traits. Any way you look at it, your creative leadership skills will be the sum of your experiences—good and bad.

---

**Flashback**   When I arrived in San Antonio, TX, I worked for one of the most difficult CDs I've ever met. Honestly, I am amazed that he is still in business today. When I was employed by him, he was negative, overbearing, demanding, and rude. No one was immune to his unprofessional behavior. He had a strict view of what the office culture had to be and how quickly jobs should be completed. While quick-turn jobs occur from time to time in the industry, every project he assigned has incredibly tight and almost unrealistic deadlines.

Music could not be played in the office and any talking had to be kept to a minimum. If there was any talking in the office, it could only be about the projects we were working on. He was the type of person you did not want to get upset for fear of his explosive temper and demeaning behavior toward the person who dared disappoint him.

I recall working on an event poster. After about an hour, I thought it was coming along nicely. I chose an energetic, yet very legible font. The color palette was appropriate for the message and style of the piece. The imagery was fantastic—at least so I thought. He passed my workstation, glanced at what I was working on, and blew a gasket. He yanked the mouse from my hand and proceeded to begin making edits to the file while standing over me. I was trapped. He had me pinned between the chair I was in and my desk. All I could do was sit there while he grumbled and complained about how horrible the design was and how long it had taken me to get to this point. Thankfully, this individual's behavior did not negatively affect my leadership style. If anything he showed me how *not* to lead a team.

---

My leadership style is based on my experience in the US Air Force. The military requires that all enlisted personnel who progress through the ranks be given specific training to help them acclimate into leadership. When I was promoted from Airman First Class (E-2) to Senior Airman (E-3), I was required to attend Noncommissioned Officer Preparatory Course (NCO Prep School).

NCO Prep School was a two-week training in which Air Force personnel were required to attend courses that focused on specific topics such as Air Force history, customs and courtesies, sexual harassment, leadership, and supervisory skills. We discussed counseling team members, motivating and leading teams, discipline, and resource allocation.

Upon reaching the rank of E-5, I attended NCO Leadership School. Similar to NCO Prep School, Leadership School provided more intensive training in the same topics that were discussed during Prep School, but there was a greater emphasis placed on teaching leadership and supervisory skills.

In hindsight, I can see how the training impacted the way in which I supervise and lead teams today. As a result of my experience with military training, I strongly believe supervisory training can help up-and-coming or new creative leaders guide their teams. I also believe it can help less-than-stellar supervisors improve their leadership skills.

What many people might not understand is that the CD or creative lead is really a conductor. She must marshal her teammates and vendors to ensure that jobs are not only created, but they are done as effectively and timely as possible. If you are not a leader, if you don't have good supervisory skills, this will be extremely difficult for you and could potentially lead to a downfall.

## Flexibility

One of the most valuable skills that I believe a creative manager should have—beyond the obvious design skills—is flexibility. Nothing goes according to plan. Each creative task can prove to be unique. As the manager, you must be able to think on your feet and solve problems quickly and effectively.

There will be times that things go smoothly and projects flow in and out of your department without a hitch. Unfortunately, that is usually not the norm. You will encounter challenges in almost every medium and on most assignments. I don't necessarily feel this is a bad thing. Responding to challenges helps us grow. If the challenges did not present themselves to be solved, then anyone could do what we do. Call it a little job security.

A challenge can come in the form of file size requirements. For example your team just finished a series of web banners for a client. The banner average in file size from 60 to 80kb, but after being submitted to the media department, you receive a message stating that the max size of submitted web banners is no larger than 40kb. What the hell?! Now you've got to quickly get with your creative and see how the banners can be decreased in size without losing clarity in the images or sacrificing the message. By the way, there is the added pressure that are you are close to missing your deadline.

Another huge challenge can be broadcast. Say you've finished recording several TV spots. You go to the production company to do post-production and realize a shot that the client has requested isn't as good as you'd like it to be. Maybe there are advertising stickers on a vehicle that must be removed from the shot. Now what? There is neither the time nor the budget to reshoot. It's time to get with your production company and come up with a solution that can be done quickly and in a way that is not painfully obvious to viewers.

Flexibility and an open mind can keep you from having an aneurism. The best creative managers make things looks easy. Presenting a cool composed front is key to keeping your team from freaking out.

# From Creative Doing to Creative Leading

What is it that certain people have that helps them get into leadership positions? In our career field it's rarely a case of nepotism. Some creatives seem to rise to the top. They are the biggest personalities in the room. What are those traits or characteristics that get people into leadership positions within the creative industry? In my experience, the trajectory that typically takes a creative to the top is their ability to not only do their job, but do it effectively. They are the ones that take the extra step to ensure that things are done right and are willing to take on additional responsibilities, as needed.

Allow me to paint the picture for you. Hey sound guy! Cue the harp...

# The Story of a Young Hungry Creative

Imagine a young, hungry creative who is ready to challenge the expected. She comes up with great ideas. She always carries a sketchbook to capture any ideas that come to her. Her book is full of concepts that she has dreamed up on her off-time. Her time off is spent refilling her well of creativity with trips to museums, socializing with friends, and enjoying community events around town. She is a voracious reader and tries to keep up on trends that affect the industry. When she is in the office, she is focused on her work and interacts with the other members of the team when they come together to brainstorm ideas or need help. After a brainstorm session, the team decides to break and come back a day later with concepts. Our driven creative returns with several ideas that not only respond to the creative brief but have been expanded to multichannel executions, extending her ideas into communications plans that effectively reach the target demographic.

This is the case every time she gets together with others to brainstorm and develop ideas. She always returns with good, targeted ideas that are strategic and effective. The team knows they can always count on her. Soon, her supervisor looks to her to lead the brainstorms. They begin to invite her to presentations. She gets invited to present during new business pitches. She continues to grow and develop, and before you know it, they promote her.

What's wrong with that? Well, our creative girl was promoted based on her ability to develop her ideas into successful campaigns. That's great because as a leader she will need to continue to do so. However, she never learned how to lead a team. When she developed her ideas, she did so on her own. Alone. She stayed in her creative bubble and only worried about the jobs she was assigned to. Now that she has been promoted and placed in a supervisory role, her charge has changed from not only developing creative ideas to also leading creatives. This is where many new creative leaders fail. If she does not expand her knowledge to go beyond being a creative doing to being a creative leading, things may not go well for her.

Since she has never learned to lead a team, she will try to do everything herself. When an issue arises, rather than discussing the issue with her team and getting them to work through the problem, she will get back into her comfort zone, jump onto the computer, and make the edits herself. If someone needs to be counseled for being late multiple times, or even substandard performance, she might either avoid conflict so she doesn't have to have the difficult conversation or she might handle it inappropriately, causing conflict between herself and her team member.

Where is she lacking? Leadership. Supervisory skills. Communication. While I do not profess that this book satisfies the requirements of old-fashioned experience and education, it will at least provide an avenue for you to start considering what parts of your own creative path need to be worked on so you can be a great creative leader.

To gain the experience and knowledge needed to be a great creative leader, I am not advocating that you should enroll in business or leadership courses. While these are definitely good ideas and would absolutely help you, I strongly believe that doing work on your own and being open to learning can lead you to be a great creative leader.

Ready? Let's roll.

## Creative Direction: Defined

Creative direction incorporates many different tasks, such as art direction, messaging, and strategy. You will find there is a fluid meaning to the title depending on where it is being used. A company may believe they have a need for an art director, but they really need a CD. Worse yet, a person is hired as a CD without a team to lead and their daily tasks really define them more as a senior designer.

Given that creative direction needs a combination of art direction, communication, and strategy, it's important to take some time and summarily define each of those terms:

- *Art Direction/Design:* The overall appearance of an object and how it visually communicates, stimulates moods, contrasts elements, and psychologically appeals to a target audience. It is the visceral ability for an object to evoke or suggest images, memories, and emotions. The physical or literal aspects of a piece of work.

- *Messaging:* What voice will you use for the copy? Will your audience understand the copy? How long will the headlines be? Will messaging be in long or short form?

- *Strategy:* a plan of action or policy designed to achieve a major or overall aim.

The primary concern of good creative direction is making sure that all three elements—art direction/design, messaging, and strategy—address issues that affect the client's bottom line.

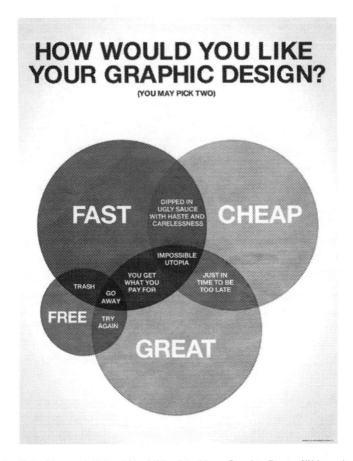

**Figure 1-1.** Colin Harman's "How Would You Like Your Graphic Design?" Venn diagram (©2009 Colin Harman)

This situation is much like the elegantly summarized Venn diagram on graphic design created by Colin Harman (see Figure 1-1). Colin's satirical take on the dilemma faced by graphic designers displays what he believes designers should provide to clients when they begin to discuss project budgets, timelines, and design parameters.

In contrast to Colin's Graphic Design Venn, when creative leaders work with their teams to ideate projects or campaigns, all three elements—art direction/design, messaging, and strategy—must be in alignment (see Figure 1-2). If any of those pieces are not considered and integrated during the ideation process, the work may fail to achieve its intended goal. That's poor creative direction. You can have a brilliant strategy and art direction, but if the messaging is not on target, that's poor creative direction. You can have appropriate art direc-

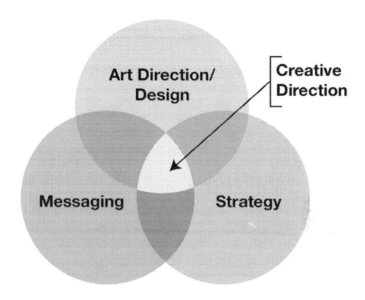

**Figure 1-2.** Creative direction diagram

tion and clever messaging, but if the strategy's not sound, that's poor creative direction. Get it?

# The CD

For many creatives, the position of CD is the ultimate goal along his or her career path. As designers increase in skills and abilities, he will move up to art director. The next step for an art director is to move up to be CD. While the path sounds valid, unfortunately there are complications.

No matter what discipline a CD comes from, his or her biggest responsibility is to ensure the quality of all disciplines under their purview. This will be a problem for any new CD who only focuses on their particular specialty. You can't be a CD with a specialty in design who doesn't understand web design or copywriting. If a CD doesn't know enough to be conversant and have the ability to lead and supervise their team they will fail. Great CDs understand each segment of a creative assignment and can push every member of their team to produce great work.

In addition to leading, CDs also have additional responsibilities such as mentoring creative team members, hiring and firing individuals, uncovering and guiding a vision for each project, building and/or maintaining a positive office culture, and more.

# Tips to Prepare for Creative Leadership

When you become the creative lead, it doesn't just involve a change in job titles, it also involves changing how you think and developing work strategies that will help you in your new role. Some of the biggest challenges you'll face will come from your coworkers. The people who have been around you and have seen you develop will sometimes be slow to accept your new role. It could be that they have a hard time shifting their perception of you, or the worst-case scenario is that they are resentful or jealous of your promotion. The following are several tips to help ease you into your new role. Recently, I had the good fortune to interview Elizabeth Grace Saunders, author of *The 3 Secrets to Effective Time Investment* (McGraw-Hill, 2013). She has written several posts on creative management, artist evolution, and scheduling, just to name a few. She provided great insight that helped me round out these tips.

## Congratulations, you've been promoted. Now what?

Now that you're the creative lead, you must change the dynamic of the relationships you have with your team. Your thoughts must now move from thinking about only yourself, to thinking more holistically about the entire team. Now you have the added responsibility of not only thinking about your own work, you must add team schedules, their varied personalities and work styles, along with directing them.

Additionally, you now must be available to your team to answer questions, help solve creative problems, and ensure that they have the resources they need to get their jobs done. The final thing you'll need to do—and possibly the most important—is providing your team with clarity regarding their jobs and their responsibilities along with outlining your expectations for them regarding your expectations on output, timelines, deliverables, and so on.

## How do you manage?

Now that you're responsible for others, part of your time each week will involve management. Regardless of team size, you will need to develop skills to juggle your new duties while having the time to successfully manage your team. Chances are you won't be thrown into managing a large team right off the bat. It will most likely be a gradual progression. As your team grows the amount of time you spend on management will increase.

Managing others well is not a waste of time. This is one of the key points that CDs usually don't value. They want to keep taking care of themselves and they lose sight of one of their most valuable resources—their team. The proper management of personnel is key for your agency, studio, or organization. Make it a priority to meet with your team and provide them with direction and feedback so they can move forward.

Poor creative leaders will see their staff members' needs as obstacles to the "real work" that needs to happen and avoid spending time on them until they are forced to do so.

## Taking care of more than yourself

Understand that you will now need to juggle multiple tasks throughout the day. In addition to knowing what you have on your own plate, you will also need to know what your team is working on. You need to keep track of what your people are doing, have a grasp of the needs and goals of every client, know if there are any personnel issues to take care of... and the list continues to grow.

You need to try and keep a balance of everything so you don't end up working yourself to death. You will absolutely need to consider lowering the number of projects you expect to accomplish personally. Because you are now leading the team, you can't expect to have enough time to produce many elements. Here's some insight from Elizabeth:

> When you move to a CD role, you need to realize that your focus must shift from doing to leading. That means more time spent on planning work, communicating vision, giving feedback, and developing staff. Given that higher level of people management, you'll need to reduce your expectations around how much project work you can do yourself. If you don't, you'll end up frustrated because you'll end up working two jobs and not feel like you're doing a great job at either.
>
> —Elizabeth Grace Saunders,
>
> author of The 3 Secrets to Effective Time Investment

## Have some "groove time"

As a creative lead, interruptions will become the norm, so you will need to set boundaries. I used to have something called "groove time." This was a period of the day when I would not answer any e-mails or even pick up the phone. It was specific time during the day that was carved out for me to concentrate on my projects—those items that required my undivided attention. To be able to have your own "groove time" you will need to set some boundaries.

Several viable options you might consider include closing your office door (if you have one) during certain times of the day, shutting down e-mail alerts for a few hours, or marking your calendar as busy. If you work in an office with an open floor plan, consider putting up a "Do Not Disturb" sign on your monitor. The method you use is not as important as setting intentional focused time to be able to move forward your own projects instead of only supporting your people on their activities.

Keep in mind, if you set time for yourself every day, you are not neglecting your responsibilities as the creative leader. In fact, you are doing exactly what you need to do. You are responsible for more than the creative output for your department. You may also be responsible for ensuring departmental budgets and profitability goals are maintained, supplies, communication with vendors, supervision and leadership of your team, or any other number of tasks. These are all elements that are part of the CD gig and must be accomplished in order for you to succeed. If you merely jump from creative project to creative project without paying attention to all of the additional responsibilities of creative leadership, you may soon find yourself out of a job.

---

▦ **Note**   I will get to brainstorming and concentration in a subsequent chapter, but before I do I wanted to quickly touch on distractions. You will never be able to do your best work if you are constantly stopping to answer e-mails as soon as they chime in. To do your job effectively, you will need to be strict about keeping to your preferred communication methodology. Set aside a dedicated time each day to respond to e-mail. Try not to live in the continually filling inbox. Strive to cluster all of your communication into dedicated blocks of time. Consider scheduling ten minutes at the beginning of each hour to address the e-mails in your inbox.[1] This technique can help you stay focused on the task at hand rather than being interrupted by the needs, wants, and demands of others.

---

[1] Todd Henry, *The Accidental Creative: Being Brilliant at a Moment's Notice* (New York: Penguin Group, 2011), 100.

# Set Expectations

When you begin your trek into leadership, understand that you can't do everything for everyone. You have to set expectations so everyone—from clients to teammates—will understand what you can accomplish. If you can't do something, let them know. It's much better to be honest with someone and let them know what you will be able to deliver than to promise something and fail to deliver.

In terms of your team, find out what type of communication they would like to receive from you. According to Saunders, you should also discuss the most effective way to communicate to minimize interruptions. Once you agree to a format, it's important to follow through and do what you say. If you promise to meet with them weekly, do it. If e-mail is the best form of communication or they prefer other methods like IM or Slack, make it happen.

The most effective means of communication could mean a daily stand-up to address the main questions for the day or setting—and keeping—a weekly one-on-one with your direct reports. If daily check-in meetings are the choice, have them but maintain a strict time limit.

# Delegate

There is an ebb and flow in successful teams. You should not only give support but also receive support. That means where you can, give your team what I call "*management opportunities*." If someone else can handle a task that you absolutely don't need to take care of, let someone else do it. This not only frees up time for you, but increases their skills and self-confidence. Consider passing off these types of activities:

- Taking meeting minutes
- Following up on work
- Doing research on fonts
- Contacting clients to get questions answered
- Drafting up ideas
- Scheduling travel
- Training other staff members

- Delegating any part of a project that doesn't absolutely need your involvement

- Searching for photographers, printers, production companies, and so on.

With the right strategies, you can thrive in your role as a creative manager. The aforementioned items are only the tip of the iceberg. In the following chapters you will get more specific tips on how to work your way up to being a great creative leader.

# In a Nutshell

It takes a certain desire and drive to be a great creative lead. To be a great creative leader you must be someone who loves the creative process. From research to brainstorm sessions, thumbnails to drafts, revisions to final products, you really must have a desire to see projects through from the initial meeting with the client all the way through unveiling your team's work to the public.

Great creative leaders must also have a brilliant creative mind, an eye for spotting talent, and the charisma to lead your team through good times and bad. They constantly try improve themselves and motivate those around them to do the same. Several questions you must be able to answer:

- Can you be the person who other creatives want to follow, and for whom they will strive to always do their best work?

- Do you have a *passion* for new ideas and a relentless *drive* to make them real?

- Do you have great taste?

- Do you have a sense of what it takes to connect with the audience?

- Can you push ideas that engage or excite while remaining relevant?

- Can you help your team take good ideas and make them great?

Keep in mind that everyone's creative journey is unique. Subsequent chapters will break down specific skills you can work on whether you are a midlevel creative who desires to make it to the mountaintop or a senior-level creative who simply wants to refresh the skills they already have. Read through the chapters and see what will work for you.

If you want this, all you have to do is work for it. You can do it. #wepa

# Leading a Creative Team

## Why do some creatives make it to the top?

Don't get hung up on the titles presented in this book. Titles vary from agency to agency, studio to studio, or in-house department to in-house department. In some places a creative director will accomplish the same tasks as a senior art director and vice versa. You will find that responsibilities and titles are somewhat interchangeable based on the size of the company you're working for and the type of work they do.

Regardless of what the company calls them now, a creative lead takes overall responsibility for the function of the creative department. For the purposes of this book I will use creative director and creative lead interchangeably.

When someone becomes creative lead, it will necessitate an entirely different skill set than the one that got them there. You may be worried about either not being a good leader or not being a good creative; don't sweat that. If you put the time and effort into it, you can become a great creative director. The key is that you must be dedicated to doing it.

Some creatives have a knack for leadership. They willingly accept responsibility when needed. From taking the extra steps needed to ensure that a client's project fulfills the assignment parameters to communicating any difficulties that will impact the timeline before it's too late, there are creatives who

© Eleazar Hernández 2017

E. Hernández, *Leading Creative Teams*, DOI 10.1007/978-1-4842-2056-6_2

just seem to have a knack for leadership. When you make it to creative lead (whether it's as a creative director or another leadership title) you become the person in charge of the overall success (or failure) of the department.

# Qualities of a Great Creative Leader

Besides having your base skills that got you to the job—graphic design, art direction, copywriting, web development, and so on—you must develop holistic skills as an account planner, account handler, social media expert, and strategic visionary. Your days will turn into marathon meetings, brainstorm sessions, client presentations, new business pitches, just to name a few. You will have to learn how to train, develop, and trust your creative team to produce work that you can review and direct. You need to develop a new vision. An all-encompassing vision that allows you to see the big picture to solve a client's communications challenge. The days of focusing on whether a color is PMS 186 or PMS 187 are over. Now you have to depend on your team to take care of that. So what are the qualities of a great creative leader?

## Love What You Do

If you don't love what you're doing, how can you pass that love or desire on to your team? How can you keep them motivated when a client is driving you crazy? There is nothing worse than a prima donna creative leader who is stuck in the past. They always relive their "glory days" and keep referring to techniques or ideas they have used in the past. A great creative leader stays up to date with current trends, techniques, and life in general. They are excited about the future and how they can work with their team to expand each client's creative.

## Have Great Taste

One of the main qualifications to be a creative director is to have a track record of great work. Experienced creatives also have a keen ability to spot great work as it's being developed. This is a key skill that a creative must develop if they want to someday lead a creative team successfully. It's important that a creative lead have a track record of success because it helps with their authority over the creative team. Which creative team member wants to follow a leader who doesn't have a history of producing great work?

Unfortunately the only way to develop a good eye is through work and research. You must be a student of your craft and always explore outside of your comfort zone. Working at your current job and only paying attention to what happens within the confines of your current clients will lead to mediocre ideas and limited conceptual ability. If you are a print creative, explore the digital realm. If you focus on digital, see what you can learn from social media marketers.

I am not saying that you need to spend every waking hour reviewing award publications and web sites to gain an understanding of what is good. In fact, I recommend to creatives that I have worked with that they absolutely not rely on publications like *Communication Arts*, *HOW*, Lurzer's Archive or *PRINT* for inspiration. To rely on those publications—although I love them and subscribe to those and several others—is to be inspired by something that was concepted and created a year ago. Of course you should look at them to see what *has* been done, or to check out who is winning what; just don't be handcuffed into being directly inspired by them.

I recommend signing up for e-blasts like AdAge, Creativity, or Ads of the World and reviewing what they are showcasing because they are much more current. In addition to studying what's going on in the industry, you should look outside of what others are doing to get a more well-rounded view of the world so that it informs your eye and your conceptual abilities when you are brainstorming alone or with your team.

## Speak the Lingo

Creative directors should be versed in several disciplines. They should understand business landscape of their client, as well as understand the brand at a deeper level. They should be versed in everything about the client's brand: audience, demographics, products, services, distribution, and so on. Having this foundation of understanding will help define the strategy.

Being able to talk about design—to communicate why something *is* working versus why something *is not*, is an integral skill for a creative director to have (Figure 2-1).

**Figure 2-1.** To communicate with your team you must know their language.

Many of us can discuss the intricacies of things such as typography, white space, and information architecture, but being able to explain the visual process or design principles that led to the solution is something that even many junior and midlevel visual creatives struggle with. Being able to explain design to an internal audience is one thing, but a creative lead must be able to coherently communicate the visual direction to a client.

In general, I believe that depending on what specialty a creative lead originates, they should develop a working knowledge of the other disciplines that they will need to speak to. Like all other disciplines, what I'm recommending is a working knowledge to be able to ask the right questions, and ideally, know when there's something you don't know.

Some people believe that ignorance is bliss and if you don't know about the other fields, you won't be limited by what they can and can't do. The problem is that, as a creative lead, all the different specialties that make up the items you offer your clients are now within your periphery.

## Champion Someone Else's Work

Championing someone else's work is not something that creatives naturally do. Our goal is to create work that is original. As a creative myself, I know firsthand that we creatives have egos. We not only learn how to do our jobs, we strive to do them to the best of our ability. Because we put so much effort into our jobs, we like to receive a little credit for the work we put into every project for every account. We get into the business because we love being creative. As a new creative lead or someone who is trying to make their way up the ranks, you will need to work on becoming a champion for others as well, and believe me it's not that easy.

## Enjoy Watching Others Create Great Things

You can't be one of those creative leaders who only likes to work on the cool assignments. When it's time to work on TV spots in Miami or direct a photo shoot with celebrities, they leave their team behind to work on the less glamorous jobs. To be successful as a creative lead, you must allow your people to not only create great things, but to also participate in fun things. Step back far enough that your team feels they are being trusted to take responsibility for a creative assignment, but remain close enough that you can assist them if they need help. You can be your team's greatest source of wisdom and support.

## Give Away Your Ideas

There will be times when your team is either floundering or off-target and you will have to come to the rescue. Those are the times when you will have to do something most creatives hate to do—give your ideas away to be developed by others. We treat our ideas like proprietary information. The ideas are our babies. Those cute little sparks of inspiration that we nurture, feed, and grow into campaigns. Our ideas are personal—they came from our minds and represent a little piece of our soul—so it's difficult to simply give them away for others to develop. What's worse is if the idea you've given away is developed in a direction that is not what you originally had in mind. Suck it up, Buttercup. This is just another aspect of trusting your team, the same way championing their ideas is. While this seems like something that will be difficult (because it will), you will get used to it. So put that tissue away and stop waving goodbye to your little ideas. C'mon now. You can do it.

## Defend Your Team and the Work

*Team:* Your team should feel they will be protected by you. Don't get me wrong, this protection does not give them carte blanche to do whatever they want. Your protection is meant to give them a safe place to share ideas while keeping them inspired and shielded from any detractors before a concept is fully realized. When you protect your team, they should feel that they have the freedom to progress through their creative process without fear.

*Work:* When it's time to present your team's work to internal teams and then to the client, you must be prepared to defend it. Before stepping in to present, be sure you have a firm understanding of the process that led the team through the conceptual exploration and development of the creative.

## Be a Mentor

Creatives that lack drive and ambition won't produce great work. If your team is filled with unmotivated individuals, you will eventually fail as their creative lead. One of your key responsibilities is to develop a team of creatives professionals who might someday take your job. If you have junior and midlevel creatives who are only producing work, and do not feel as if they have any kind of trajectory to improve their job skills, or to advance to the next level in their career, you will soon find them performing poorly or simply leaving for a new career opportunity.

Take the time to nurture your creatives and help them grow. It will only benefit you to do so. You will have earned their loyalty because they will know that you are invested in them.

## Always Strive to Do Better Work

Honestly, it will be rare that your creatives will show up at a brainstorm session with ideas that do not need to be tweaked. Although you don't want to be too harsh or callous, don't beat around the bush and waste everyone's time. Kill the ideas that aren't going to work. While I do not condone insulting or berating anyone, I do believe that as professionals, we owe it to one another to be honest.

If you don't believe a concept is on-target or strategically sound, kill it. That said, be sure to inspire and encourage your team to do better. Push them to explore further and dig beyond the surface.

## Be a Great Presenter

I'll deal with this in the Chapter 8, but understand that without the ability to sell your ideas, you won't go far. Get ready for public speaking. Lots of it.

## Be a Good Listener

Listen. Really listen. It's the only way to understand what a client's challenges as well as what they are thinking. I'm not a huge talker in meetings. If the client has requested the meeting, I believe I am there to hear what they have to say. I listen, ask questions as needed, and summarize as we begin to bring the meeting to a close. I am not at the meeting to interrupt them or finish their sentences. I am there to listen and interpret what they are saying so I can relay that information to my team. Try it. Sit quietly in your next meeting and see how much you can pick up.

## Share

Don't be paranoid about sharing your knowledge and expertise, even with competitors. I'm not saying that you should share agency secrets, but if a fellow creative director calls you for help, help them. In the end, we're in this together. You never know when you might be in need of their help.

You can also give by sharing your experience and expertise with the world. Try writing blogs, speaking at conferences, presenting to college classes, entering competitions, and so on. There are plenty of opportunities mentioned to get yourself out there.

## Stand for Something

It's easy to be liked. You just have to be accommodating and not have any conviction. This is definitely fair-weather creative direction. Keep leading this way and your work and team will be average—otherwise known as *lame*. Hold yourself and your team to higher standards. Expect the best from them. If they don't meet your expectations, don't sweat it. As long as they are trying to reach them.

There will be times when you must call someone to task. You may have to have uncomfortable conversations with your team to let them know they need to step it up. You are not being paid to be liked. You are being paid to lead your team. Do it. Lead them. Just make sure you do it respectfully, and after the dust settles, be sure to recognize when they get back in line with what you're expecting.

## Believe

Doesn't it just suck when a project is presented by someone who doesn't really get it? They should be expressing the emotional intensity of the spot, but they sound more like the teacher from *Ferris Bueller's Day Off*. If the presenter doesn't believe in the work, why would the audience care? Once you have committed to a creative route, defend it. Believe that it is the greatest idea on the planet—and make a stand for that work.

This list of creative leader traits could go on and on. Some of them are obvious, or at least I think they are. I believe that the stereotypical example of a creative director is rare. If those people actually existed they would be extremely difficult to work with.

Now that we've gone over the traits you should display, let's look at the types of team members you will lead.

# Potential Creative Team Personalities

Creatives are an interesting bunch. The things that make us unique are also the things that make us challenging to work with. Adjectives used to describe creative personalities include moody, excitable, perfectionistic, sloppy, talkative, distracted, egotistical, shy, gossipy, impulsive, quiet, and so on. I know what you're thinking, "This could describe pretty much any group of people in any career field." Sure. It could. What if I told you all of those adjectives describe a single person? Sure, I'm exaggerating a bit... sort of. I can tell you from firsthand experience, we are a very emotional bunch. Because of this, as the creative lead responsible for your team, you have to learn how to work with a wide variety of people with varied (and sometimes multiple) personalities.

While there is no magic formula or standardized way to work with every creative team, there is something you can do. You need to have an understanding of the types of personalities you will have on your team. This is not meant to be a list of every personality you'll face. It's just a sampling.

## "Keep Me Informed" Team Member

Some people like to be kept in the loop. They want to know everything that is going on and how that affects their portion of the project. They want to brainstorm in groups. They thrive when multiple people provide input and ideas. These individuals don't mind sharing the spotlight. As a matter of fact, they would like a large spotlight that will shine over everyone.

There is one main drawback: they won't make decisions on their own. If a decision needs to be made their first instinct is to try to solicit input from others. They don't want to make the decision on their own because they feel they lack the authority to do so or they are afraid of the repercussions if others don't agree or things go south.

This type of worker needs attention and definitely requires parameters to work within. If you'd like them to make decisions, you will have to provide them with the decisions to make. Give them an idea of the pros and cons of each decision, and then let them know you will support their decision no matter which one they choose. The key to taking this route is to ensure that you, as the creative lead, are comfortable with the options you offer to them so that you will be happy with whatever direction they choose to go.

## "Get Out of My Way" Team Member

There are team members who prefer the autonomy to work alone. While they enjoy working with the group, at times they prefer to work alone to gather their thoughts, research ideas, sketch comps, or simply to think and develop their ideas with a trusted partner.

The problem with these types of team members is they may rush to a decision because they are eager to prove that they can do things on their own. Because of this their concepts may not be as developed as those who work in pairs or groups. This may occur in part because they do not have a sounding board to bounce their ideas off of. However, there are "loners" who have the ability to create great work in solitude and without the benefit of another set of eyes.

The key is to understand their level of creative ability. Do they think strategically to come up with solutions that are not only visually pleasing, but that satisfy the parameters of the project? Or do they develop creative and try to shove ideas for the client into an idea or concept they have seen done in the past? Either way, you must reinforce to these creatives that they must keep you informed of their progress so they do not develop creative too far and risk being off-target.

## "Life Isn't Fair! Why Can't I Do That?!" Team Member

Occasionally you will have to deal with a team member that thinks the world is their enemy. Whether they are complaining because the client doesn't like their proposed color palette or do not understand the design provided, these creatives will have something to say. They will complain, whine, and mumble about everything. How do you deal with that? I have worked with some leads who believe the best way to deal with this kind of team member is to fire them before they poison the rest of the team. While "kicking them to the curb" has its merits, I prefer to at least take a stab at changing negative behavior.

If someone is a constant complainer, there has to be a basis for their rumblings. What is it that is making them find the negative in every situation? A series of questions that you should ask yourself before taking action are as follows: Has this person always been like this? Is this a sudden change of behavior? Are their rumblings unfounded, or are there many reasons for them to act the way they do? Are you able to positively influence them to change? Are they willing and able to change? Will they be receptive to constructive criticism?

As a creative leader, it's not your job to dig into their personal lives to discover if something else is instigating their behavior. But if it's impacting their ability to do their job, you may be able to encourage them to take steps to address those issues before it results in them losing their job. Try to motivate them and give them some positive support. Encourage them to make positive changes. In the end it's up to them to decide if they want to change.

On the other hand, if—one, you don't want to bother or two, you really don't care—then move forward with recommending their dismissal and start finding someone who will complement your existing team. I would also recommend not finishing this book because you're really not interested in becoming the best creative leader you can be.

## "I Need to Be Told What to Do" Team Member

This type of team member is the one that you will have to work with to teach them how to self-motivate and take the initiative. You will have to try and break through the barriers they put up. Whether it's fear of taking on too much responsibility, fear of stepping on someone's toes, fear of not knowing what to do, or worse yet just plain laziness, this is the team member that needs to be given specific directions. This team member can lead to some very exasperating moments for you. While everyone else on the team may be humming along and getting lots of work done, this member will do exactly what they are told. Nothing more. They will wait for your direction to move forward on every project.

At first you may think this is a good thing. It feels as if this person has a strong sense of loyalty and they want to execute your vision to the letter. Then you are slapped in the face with reality when you just don't have time to deal with them. You don't have the luxury of sitting down and explaining every little nuance of every assignment. You can't control every move of their mouse or make every decision for them. Should they use Helvetica or Avenir? Should they use PMS 186C Red or PMS 200C Red? Should the headline 18 point or 24 point? You don't have time to handhold your team members. You need to get this personality type trained to think for themselves—quickly.

# Desired Team Members

There is no set formula for the perfect team. You want to have a team of people that are willing to learn and do not constantly question decisions. You want the best designers, the best art directors, the best copywriters, and so on. You should build a team of creative experts or creatives who have the potential to quickly become experts. When hiring, sometimes it's not about the resume, it's about the personality and drive that the person possesses.

Whenever possible, you want to hire people that know more than you about a particular field of expertise. When each person has something special to add to the mix, you could have a great team that produces amazing work. The best work will come from a group of motivated, creative individuals who do their jobs and can be led to work in harmony with the rest of the creative team.

# Mentoring a Creative Team

It's one thing to lead a creative team. It's a completely different thing to mentor creative team members. Mentoring your team takes time—time that you might not feel you have or even want to spend. However, it's important to nurture the relationship you have with your team. They will be driven to do their best work if they feel you are invested in them. Now, this isn't a plea for long walks in the park or even special one-on-one lunches. This is a strong recommendation that you take a vested interest in each member of your team's career and skill development.

Some of the lessons a team can learn will be ones you can share with them. There are mistakes you've made along the way that you can help them avoid. Mistakes that may have cost you (or your agency) money. Mistakes that have caused you a little embarrassment. From my own experience, I can remember a $1,600 typo on a small run brochure. The $1,600 was the cost of a new print run. Granted the client had to absorb some of the blame for the typo getting through the proofing process, but in the end the fingers were pointed at the design team, and we had to eat the cost.

Never mentored anyone before? This is another "management opportunity" for you. Allow me to help get you started. Here are some tips and thought starters for you to share with your current or future mentees:

## You should always do your best work.

Be mindful of any creative decision you make. Once made, stick with it. You may be tempted to do a half-assed job or just go through the motions from time to time. Great creatives can take a good job and make it great. This will consistently be a big challenge for you. There will be clients who are just out-right pains-in-the-ass. Suck it up. Lead your team the way they should be led. Understand the challenge ahead of you and do the best you can. Get it done.

## Spend time learning about your client.

Really spend time learning about them. What makes them tick? What are their products and services? What is their mission statement? Who are their customers? What is their ownable brand idea? What makes them better than anyone else? It does no good to come up with concepts that either don't work or have been done. Get to know and understand your client.

## Build a network of trusted contemporaries.

Your creative team should not simply insulate themselves with their coworkers. They should get out into the world and make connections. Those connections will serve them well in the future. Whether it's to get advice, serve as a sounding board, or be a safe place where they can compare their creative leaders. Every creative needs compatriots who they can commiserate with. Be open to pay it forward as well. Give of yourself to help your friends or those who ask for your help.

## Be honest. Really honest.

Being honest doesn't mean rude. Being honest also doesn't mean you should tiptoe around issues. There is nothing worse than listening to someone try to give constructive criticism, only to meander around the main issues because they are afraid of hurting feelings. Give me a break. We are all adults. Be honest, but don't make it personal. You can tell someone their design is not good without insulting their momma!

## If you want to be good at what you do, work at it.

For many of us, being creative, strategic-minded, and on-target is a skill that is developed over time. You have to live advertising. It not something you turn on or off from 8 to 5. You live it all the time. Being observant of life around you will help inform your creative. We are informed by what we see, read, watch, and so on. Small things that we do or see can become big ideas in the next great campaign, but you have to work for it. Be observant. Do the work.

## Be honest with yourself. Don't show crap work.

Let your mentees know that everyone can spot an idea that isn't well-developed. If they can't explain an idea so everyone immediately gets the key insight, then it might not be worth the time. Or worse yet, if they were asked to show up to a meeting with ideas, and show up with things they scribbled up at lunch before the meeting, let them know they should just keep it to themselves. In the brainstorm chapter I will discuss the value of having succinct brainstorm sessions that stay focused and productive. There is no time for uninspired ideas that waste time.

## Sketch. Write. Repeat.

Encourage your team to sketch their ideas out. In fact, why not get everyone on your team a sketchbook to get them started? This is something I have done with every creative team I have led. I believe that ideas can't be fully formed until the concept is developed. Too many creatives jump to the computer to try and develop ideas and get lost in the minutia of font choice, color choice, layout, and so on, before there is a good idea. Scribbling and refining by hand is the best way to get to something that should be on a computer. When your team scoffs or complains about their lack of drawing ability, remind them that they don't have to be artists and create masterpieces. They simply need to get their ideas down on paper so they can continue to develop them. Ideas written down become more tangible than those that rumble around in memory and risk being forgotten.

## Control what you can.

Other creatives might not work as hard as you do. Clients might not understand the work you show them. Account Service may feel the creative has not addressed the client's marketing challenge. Whatever the reason, sometimes your vision might not be understood or agreed with. Control what you can. Find out what they don't agree with. Provide rational reasons why you believe your creative solution is good and try to win them over. If they still don't get it, come back with something that helps assuage their concerns.

## Expect more.

Copywriters demand more of your art directors. Art directors demand more of your copywriters. Challenge each other. Many agencies partner copy and art creatives into what we call "dupla." If you're lucky your dupla partner will be just as creative, insightful, and driven as you are. If you're not lucky you will end up with a slouch who needs some motivation. Push them to work harder. Make sure the entire execution is strong, regardless of your particular specialty.

# Don't be a whiner.

We are not curing cancer. We are in a creative field. We are getting paid to create things and use our imaginations. Remember that when you are whining about a client not liking the color you chose. Screw it. Pick another one. Think about it. We get to draw, pick type, decide colors, write headlines, art direct TV spots, work on radio spots, code websites. We have it pretty good. Enjoy it. Appreciate it. Think about something that pissed you off last week or last month. Does that even matter to you today? Are you still losing sleep over it? Has it impacted the world in a negative way? Of course not. Move on.

In short, you are trying to build a team of creatives who you can depend on. It does no one any good if you are constantly second guessing, revising, or changing the work that your creative team is producing. Be mindful of the role you play in their development. Guide their growth. Support their desire to expand their field of knowledge. Be a cheerleader when they succeed. Call them on the carpet when need be. Provide honest feedback and timely praise. Follow up on what you have promised them.

# In a Nutshell

Okay, finally this brings us back to what it takes to lead a creative team. What is a creative leader? Is he a mad creative genius, who thinks up great ideas or does he help to make his team's ideas better? Is she the defender of the creative vision—regardless of who created it? Bottom line, the role is defined according to the needs of the environment in which they exist. It cannot be a single definition.

Always. Always. Always remember that you can't really be a creative director or a creative lead without a team to lead. You need to have a group that you can trust and who will be loyal to you. There will be times when you will have to make difficult choices. Choices that others might not understand or agree with. This will be made easier if you have a team that trusts you.

Are there definite rules to how much experience creative leaders should have or how old they should be? In short… no. I know creative directors who are in their mid-50s and those who are in their late 20s. Whether you have experienced good CDs or bad ones, creative directors come in all shapes, sizes, levels of experience, ages, and temperaments. The bottom line is that a good creative director has the ability to distill information and transform that into creative brilliance, and deliver to the audience while maintaining a single mindedness to make that idea happen. How brilliant or successful you become will be based on what you put into the job and your willingness to learn and grow.

I became a creative director over 16 years ago. It took me almost four years to get there. I didn't rush. I didn't scramble toward it. I just did the things that I did with plenty of love, enthusiasm, attention, and plenty of coffee thrown in to help me through the all-nighters (Café Bustelo. Now comes for the Keurig! #wepa Please forgive the shameless plug.)

I've won awards for some great projects and some great brands. I remember every line, every page, every font, every color choice. I'm very proud of the work I've created, but I am most proud of the creatives I have mentored, and the teams I have helped to develop in the last 20 years. I have loved (almost) every minute of it.

# Leading an Advertising Creative Team

## Where are all the Mad Men and Women at?

A creative team in the field of advertising consists of the people who actually work to create the idea or concept that attempts to satisfy the communication challenges faced by their clients. The team has two specialties: art and copy. Advertising agencies generally refer to their resident experts in the visual and verbal as their "creative team."

The primary objective of the creative team is to develop the components of an advertising or branding campaign that creates a desire among the public for their client's product, service, or organization. When you think about it, it seems pretty obvious that there is usually a positive correlation between the amount of advertising a company or organization runs and its influence on consumers. Why? It's all about public awareness. If people don't know you're out there, how will they know to purchase your product, use your service, or support your organization? We can easily see the correlation between the amount of advertising dollars spent to promote the product and how people view a product. For example, if we were to compare the influence of

© Eleazar Hernández 2017

E. Hernández, *Leading Creative Teams*, DOI 10.1007/978-1-4842-2056-6_3

Coke products—a product with a very large advertising budget—to that of a generic local store's cola, you can be sure that Coke's influence would be significantly greater. A larger budget means more advertising and promotions leading to great influence or at least awareness among the general public. The greater awareness also helps Coke compete with any equals out there. As a matter of fact, even if they simply want to maintain their market share and remain at the same level of awareness, they would still have to put a considerable amount of money into their advertising.

Advertising creative teams also work to build brand awareness. Brand awareness, simply put, is the knowledge or understanding that the general public has of a client's brand. This awareness influences how they perceive what the brand does or what it represents. For example, let's say a relatively well-known electronics company wants to be known as a leader in the industry because of its revolutionary products. It is the responsibility of the creative team to develop a communications solution that helps lead the public toward a desired brand awareness and if everything goes well, loyalty. Alright. Enough intro. Let's jump into it. *Oui? Oui!*

# Advertising Creative Team Members

To understand how to lead this team, you must first understand who you'll have on your team and what roles they occupy. I provide one caveat with the following information. The following descriptions merely provide one way to understand the inner workings of an advertising agency creative team. There are any number of setups that can be found in agencies throughout the United States and abroad. In the end, there is one overarching truth—a creative director (CD) guides the creative team through the ideation process and helps ensure that they develop communications solutions that are strategically sound and provide accurate representation for the brands.

Most advertising agency teams maintain a hierarchy that consists of several different levels—from junior to senior level as shown in Figure 3-1. Some of the job titles utilized for team members are pretty obvious while others can to get a bit long and intimidating.

Let's take a generalized look at how a typical advertising agency creative team could be structured. For the sake of this discussion, the highest leadership level I will discuss is CD. Please understand that highest leadership position in an agency can continue up the career chain beyond the CD. There are Group CDs, Executive CDs, and Continental CDs (i.e., North American CD, Chief Creative Officer, Global Chief Creative Officer, etc.). I decided to stop at CD because there is a greater number of "regular" CDs than any of the higher CDs.

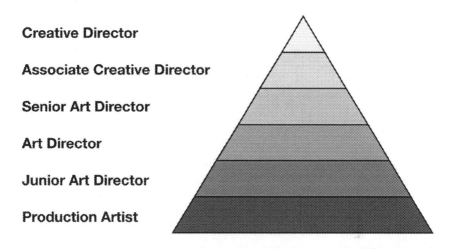

- Creative Director
- Associate Creative Director
- Senior Art Director
- Art Director
- Junior Art Director
- Production Artist

**Figure 3-1.** Agency creative department structure

# Your Team

The creative team is what makes an ad agency environment different from most other types of communication companies. The creative team works together from the beginning of the project through its completion. After reading the creative brief, they brainstorm and determine a creative path that will achieve the assignment's objectives and address a client's marketing challenges. Usually, they conceptualize visual and verbal ideas as a group (or at least as a pair) before splitting up to polish up the deliverables and then combining them into the creative whole. Let's take a look at your team.

For the following descriptions, you'll want to imagine you are listening to your favorite game show theme song. If you can't come up with a game show whose music you enjoy, insert this link into your browser (https://www. youtube.com/watch?v=UvulxN8hY6o). Once you've loaded it up, play the music and then read through the descriptions. For added fun, be sure to read them in your best "over-the-top" game show announcer voice.

## Art Director

He's one half of a creative duo. Responsible for the visual elements on a given assignment. The art director creates the layouts, selects colors, searches for stock photo imagery, and directs photo shoots. He's a master at teaming with illustrators, he easily works with freelancers, and he guides the creative work through the production process. He's often a foosball master, an avid watcher of comic book–themed movies, a lover of four-legged animals, and believes a good beer should never be adorned with fruit… heeeeeere's the art director!

# Copywriter

The other half of the creative team, the copywriter writes headlines, crafts subheads, and develops body copy. She determines if ad copy is written in first person, such as testimonials from customers, or in the third person as a narrative. She revises copy for grammar and clarity. She ensures that it all works within the format in which it's placed. She's an avid scrapbooker, a fan of Earth, Wind and Fire, and can always provide a solid argument for both sides of less filling or great taste… leeeeeeeeet's meet the copywriter!

# Traffic/Production Manager

The person who keeps the jobs moving and creatives in line. She is the facilitator of information between Account Service and the creative department. She deals with vendors to get items printed or produced. She knocks out estimates to help determine whether a five-color print job is a viable option. She has a love/hate relationship with Coke, she's a meticulous proofer, and she has a hankering for Broadway musicals… how about a big round of applause for the traffic manager!

# Additional Creative Team Members

Medium-sized agencies sometimes have a sizable creative team led by one or more creative leads. Typically each account has a CD or associate CD (ACD) as an overall creative lead. The CD or ACD will have the support of art directors and at least one copywriter. If a medium-sized agency only has one CD, she will depend on senior-level art directors to act as creative leads on agency accounts while they themselves maintain overall leadership. Because of the flexibility afforded to members of the creative team in medium-sized agencies, there will frequently be project overlap. For example, a financial account could have a senior-level art director who leads along with a copywriter and junior-level art direction support.

At times an art director will work with a different copywriter on different accounts, and vice versa. For example, Art Director A and Copywriter B could be teamed on a Hispanic supermarket account. Art Director C and Copywriter B could be teamed on a statewide social service account.

In medium-sized agencies, creative teams may mix and match. Sometimes the team make-up is determined by who is best qualified to do the work. This will be based on their past experience, their creative skills, or their interests. Other times, teams are composed of those creatives who simply have the bandwidth to take on more work. Any way you slice it, in advertising agencies of this size, there is usually enough work to keep everyone busy.

In small agencies, the creative team shares duties on several accounts. Each member will typically be assigned jobs that are suited to his or her interests or expertise. The creative lead oversees all clients while allowing the members of the creative team develop the various client assignments.

If an agency is small it will have one creative lead supervising, directing, and leading a team of creatives. That individual will be responsible for the overall creative product that leaves the office. The next level of leadership below that is typically an ACD. That position can take on any number of responsibilities. If the CD is leading the overall creative product, then the ACD is responsible for the leadership of the team members that ideate and/or produce the creative product. The ACD position shares responsibility between group leadership and supervisory responsibilities.

The ACD can sometimes be a middle-management position. ACDs straddle the line between creative production and creative leading. The ACD will begin attending more meetings while still being responsible for a certain amount of creative labor. In a perfect world, it is during this career phase that ACDs should be learning what's required to be a great CD.

Below the ACD will be several levels of art directors. The positions range from senior art director to art director to junior art director. The senior art director has some responsibility for orchestrating the different tasks needed to get creative work produced. In other words, not only will the senior art director produce work but he will be responsible for ensuring other tasks get accomplished (contacting photographers, press checks, selecting fonts, etc.). A senior art director can be one of the most senior-level creatives producing work.

The junior art director occupies an entry-level position that should be dedicated to job training. Their job is to learn as much as they can, as quickly as they can, to become contributing members of the department.

---

▓ **Soapbox Moment**    I believe one of the biggest mistakes that agencies make is giving a junior art director title to recent college graduates. Why do I think this is a mistake? Allow me to explain.

Break out the title into its components and you'll pretty much have the reason that I have a problem with assigning it to recent grads. To be an art director means that you should have the experience to actually direct something. Recent grads should have a period of time in which they are learning the basics of being a creative. They should be receiving training on things such as brainstorming, creating comps, and utilizing the tools they need to understand: Adobe InDesign, Illustrator, Photoshop, After Effects, and so on. It also takes time to unlearn some of the bad ideation or production habits acquired during school and learn good working habits that will help them through their career.

For their first job, the junior-level creative staffer should be working in the vein of a production artist. They should be helping out some of their more senior-level creative teammates by putting together comps, finishing up working documents, or searching for stock photos. They should be involved in brainstorms, attend photo shoots, tag along on press checks, sit in on client meetings, continue to familiarize themselves with the programs needed for their specific jobs, and so on. Time as a junior-level staffer should be one that is filled with learning. They should absorb as much information and get as much experience as they can.

It will take time to train junior-level creatives, and time is a precious commodity that is sometimes lacking in a creative leader's day. However, when you take on that responsibility and devote the necessary time and energy to it, you will reap the benefits. Not only will your junior creative be well-trained, but you will have the added reward of knowing that you helped someone under your charge develop and grow. Ok, I'm stepping off the soapbox… for now.

## Advertising Creative Team Objectives

The objective of any good team is to produce work that is true to the brand and relevant to the consumer. Additionally, it should be creatively fulfilling; otherwise, the team members will dread going to work every day. This is the creative trinity that will keep us all happy. However, even though we can have all three, there will always be those projects or clients with nonsensical requests and endless edits that can tempt your team to push out garbage work.

This is the reality of the gig. There will always be bread-and-butter clients that bring money into the agency, but don't allow you to spread your creative wings. Then there are the clients who will challenge your creativity and give you a little more creative license to produce groundbreaking work. Either way, your team must be able to address a client's marketing challenges with creative solutions.

The typical team in the creative department will consist of an art director and a copywriter who can work together well. It was Bill Bernbach, the founder of DDB, who first teamed art directors and copywriters in the late 1950s. Prior to this, combining these two specific talents had never been done. The idea quickly caught on and has been the standard for most advertising agencies ever since. The "*dupla*" (a term coined by Hispanic advertising agencies) is the basis of all advertising teams.

## Creating the Dupla

Many smaller agencies have one or two copywriters but several art directors. When this is the case, it's difficult to create a dupla because the copywriters must be stretched between accounts. In that case, you can still find the right pairing based on project parameters, client, and personality. Regardless of size of the agency, when putting teams together, chemistry is very important.

The good thing is, if there is no chemistry in the dupla, you'll know it very quickly. Telltale signs may be gnashing of teeth, crying, name calling, and the high likelihood of receiving an atomic wedgie. While this is not the best way to find out you've got a little dissention in the team, at least you'll know if the team will or won't get along.

What can you do about this? Mediating a conversation between the two of them to find out what's going on would be the first step. In a perfect world, you will be able to resolve any conflict. If not, separate them and reassign the job.

When you have the right team, they will balance each other out and produce great work. They feel comfortable bouncing ideas off of each other, support each other during less-inspired times, and keep each other on-task. The dupla has been a lasting concept because it plays on the strengths of each person—the art director's visual strength and the copywriter's verbal strength.

When considering putting a dupla together, it would seem obvious to put together two people who think the same, who may have the same career goals, and who get along. However, that is not completely true. What you should do is find people who can respect each other while having their own thoughts and opinions. What good does it do to have two people teamed together who think the same way? That's just doubling up the same thinking. That's lame. It limits creativity and can negatively impact the number of concepts that are presented to a client.

## Advertising Creative Team Direction: Leadership Skills

One of the most difficult things we have to do as creative leaders is to let go. That's not something that comes easy to us. One of the things that gets us to our position is our love for producing great work. Since we're all attention seekers, we also kinda like praise and awards as well. When your team is working on client assignments and you notice they are pursuing a direction that isn't strategically aligned with your client's goals, it's really difficult not to just jump in and show them exactly what you want done.

Remember, everything we do is completely subjective. What you might think is a good idea, could be completely confusing to someone else. Let your teams work through the assignment. Provide key insights where you can and encourage them to develop their ideas and allow them to blossom. Your job is to spot good ideas and eliminate bad ones, while encouraging your team to continue seeking solutions. You must develop that skill so you can quickly provide your duplas with feedback when they present their ideas to you. Don't demean or demoralize your creatives when they are missing the mark. Provide guidance and encouragement and send them on their way.

In Chapter 5, we will discuss different techniques in brainstorming, in particular the "yes, and…" technique. You can also use this technique when you are reviewing ideas with your teams. Nobody likes to be told, "No," so work to find ways to add to their creative ideas without approving bad ideas.

## How to Review Work from Your Team

As the creative lead, you will quickly learn that much of your time will be spent in meetings. If you want the work to continue in your absence, you must be sure to inform your team of the best way to keep you in the loop. Communication is one of the keys to keeping things running smoothly.

As presenters, we know that we must provide a preamble or a warm-up to clue the client into our thinking and the process that led to the creative that you'll be presenting. You can most likely have your team dispense with the lengthy preamble when they are presenting their ideas to you.

If you can get your team to quickly remind you which brief they are coming to solicit your opinion on, it will help get you in the correct frame of mind to receive the information. A simple intro statement providing you with the client name, the name of the spot, and for which medium will suffice to get you going. For example: *"Hey Eli. We're here to get your input on the summer campaign TV spot for that pizza company."* They don't need to go into a long, drawn-out explanation before you start to review the work.

When you give them your rationale for how they should show you their work, remind your team that the audience will not have the benefit of a warm-up explanation to get them to see the work clearly. All you'll want to see is the work.

Now remember, using this technique is not meant to allow you to make your team feel as if you don't care about them or the work they are doing. Don't turn this into a "I don't have time for you. Show me the work and get out" kind of situation. That can't be further from the truth.

Understand that time is a precious resource in our business. Your team should not be spending a lot of time on concept(s) that you or your client might not like. You must make time for your creatives every day. Allow them to present you scribbles, thumbnails, ideas that aren't fully formed so you can make sure their ideas are both visually strong and on-strategy so you can help them focus their time and energy appropriately.

Once they get to know you and understand your likes and dislikes and how you react to work, they will be able be more selective with the ideas they present because they will already have addressed whether the concepts are on-strategy or not. Make sure your team visits with you early and often with anything that is coherent. Not every idea has to be award-winning to be heard or presented. They simply need to be able to relay the information and give you an idea of the visual treatment.

# Playing the Game

*Playing the game* is a term used for behavior that turns regular work scenarios into games where there are winners and losers. Game players work to get the job done regardless of what it takes to do it and who they have to step over to get it done. In its less extreme form, game players set themselves apart from their coworkers by sidling up to the powers that be. This behavior frequently alienates the game player and causes dissention between them and their team members.

Game players have noses that are the appropriate shade of brown (PMS 470) and their lips are firmly planted on the gluteus of the people in power. Being a game player isn't the type of person you should aspire to be. These individuals will try to make it through the ranks at any cost—typically at the expense of someone else on their team. The problem with this type of person is while their contemporaries may see them for what they are, they appear both competent and trustworthy to management.

---

**Not-So-Hypothetical Scenario**  Imagine a CD who is working closely with his team to develop concepts for a client's brand launch. They have spent many hours together ideating and developing multiple ideas for the presentation. The team finishes the work and he gathers the elements and leaves for the presentation.

During the presentation the client is pleased and says he likes the creative shown. However, he wants something different. He believes the creative team did a good job with the concepts, but they missed the mark. While the client is speaking, the CD nods and agrees with him. The CD does not defend the work. He does not explain the research that went into the creative. He doesn't defend the creative's rationale or the agency's position. The CD sycophantically thanks the client for his amazing insight and leaves.

When he returns to his team, he expresses his frustration and complains that the client is ignorant. He blames the client for forcing the creative team to change the creative work. He laments how long the team worked and how the client doesn't appreciate anything. He tells the team if there was anything he could have done to change the client's mind he would have, but the decision was not up to him. There was nothing he could do or say to change the client's mind.

This CD is playing the game. He looks good and amenable to his client while also looking like a supportive team player to his creative team. Although he lacks a spine, he comes out shining on both sides.

---

Creating good work and being a great CD is not about playing games. It's about doing your job well without leaving a trail of hurt feelings or creating a negative work environment. You should strive to be an effective creative leader by leading your team to produce great work, without demeaning and demoralizing everyone in your path or pandering to a client's every whim.

Do you have to make the tough calls sometimes? Sure. Will you have to find ways to work with clients so they don't feel that you are talking down to them? Absolutely. Will you have to sometimes acquiesce to the client's direction even if you don't believe it's the right way to go? Yes. Are you expected to motivate your team and keep them engaged and energized with the work? You betcha. Leading your team to create great work, having friendly and profitable relationships with clients, and being a leader in the agency are all expected of you as a creative leader.

Be honest with your creative team and your agency team. Understand that you are not perfect and you will sometimes make mistakes. Set a standard of excellence, and hold yourself and others accountable. Your goal is to get the best performance out of your team. If you can do so ethically with the best of intentions while leading your creative team to great heights, everybody wins… no *games* needed.

## Getting the Best from Your Art Directors and Copywriters

Your art directors and copywriters will help you solve the communications challenges faced by your clients. They will be responsible for the visual portion of the work that is produced.

Your art directors oversee the visual style of the campaign elements. They should be great visualizers and thinkers. They will assimilate and synthesize concepts and inspiration that they gather from various sources. Your copywriters provide the voice of the brand. They provide copy in long and short form that informs, educates, or entertains the audience. They will work together to provide cohesive verbal and visual solutions.

What can you expect from your creatives? Passion. Interest. Quirkiness. If you put a dozen creatives in a room, you will find that there are a dozen different personalities. Different styles. Different techniques. Different goals. You can depend on your creatives to show up with varied ideas and visual directions—lots of them.

Because your creative team can range from junior to senior level, you can expect a wide range of job and life experience to inform their work. Junior-level creatives will need to be trained, guided, and mentored. Mid- and senior-level creatives will be invaluable assets to the department. Because of the varied levels of job and life experience they bring to the table, you need to find how to get the best from each of them and how to help them work together as a team.

Lisette Sacks, former CD at MRM/McCann in New York City, provided the following advice on how to get the best from your creative team:

> A [creative lead] should really know their teams, talk to people as individuals, and take everything into account. Some people need more encouragement and check-ins and others need to be left alone to work independently. The main thing is really to understand each person's style and adapt. It isn't always easy but it makes for better work in the end.[1]

Everyone on your team represents individual skills and experiences, likes and dislikes. You can't lump your team into a generic pile, toss work to them, and expect them to execute appropriately.

In a nutshell, treating your creatives as individuals and with respect will help motivate them to give you their best work.

## Getting the Best from Your Traffic Manager

Your traffic manager manages the flow of work that goes through the creative department. She ensures that all deadlines are met and if any adjustments to schedules need to be made.

At the onset of a job or campaign, the traffic manager will meet with the CD and account executive (AE) to discuss how they will attack it. If it's a relatively simple assignment, it will go to the team that works on their particular account. If it's a large assignment, the teams could be adjusted so the senior-level creatives are assigned to the task. In a small agency with relatively few members, the creative teams will be mixed according to the strengths or skills of the creative members. For example, if one of the agency's clients is sponsoring a 5K run, that assignment is best placed with a team whose members enjoy sports or running. If the client has sponsored a Marc Anthony concert, that might call for a different team.

In a medium-sized agency, where teams have been assigned to specific clients, when the brief comes in, the creative team will join the initial meeting with the traffic manager, CD, and AE. The same creative team will work through this new assignment.

Once the assignments have been given, the traffic manager will build a calendar with the brainstorms, milestones, creative reviews, and client presentations that need to occur. Once work begins, the traffic manager will pay close attention to the progress of the work. She will request that meetings get moved back if adequate progress is not being made, and ask for assistance from other creative team members if need be.

---

[1]Sacks, Lisette. Interview with Eleazar Hernández. Personal interview. New York City, February 18, 2016.

Once the project has been approved by the client and it's ready to go into production, the traffic manager will either assign the production to a production manager or take care of the production herself. For the purposes of this section, we will deal with print production. TV production will be discussed in Chapter 10.

The traffic manager will secure estimates from printers based on the specifications provided by the creative team. The traffic manager will be responsible for negotiating with printers and sourcing tchotchkes from vendors. In some cases, you can also depend on your traffic manager to attend press checks.

One thing to keep in mind is that your traffic managers are professional project managers. It is their job to keep the job moving. They don't provide input on the creative quality of the job. Their greatest strengths are efficiency and problem-solving.

If you work with an experienced traffic manager, she will have a wealth of information regarding past projects and budgets. If you maintain good communication with your traffic manager, she can often get more time to complete projects. If you are struggling to meet the deadlines for legitimate reasons, she will have your back and can go to Account Service to request an extension. Be good to your traffic managers; they keep everything running like a well-oiled machine.

## Working Well with Account Executives

So, what exactly do those people in Account Service do? Why do they always shoot my ideas down? What the hell gives them the right to second-guess me? Why don't they ever let me push creative, cutting-edge ideas to the client?

Simply put, account service, AEs, account handlers—whatever they are called in your agency—coordinate all agency resources to work in unison to provide successful solutions to their client's marketing challenges. They work through all phases of the process from initial planning through execution.

Many creatives feel that Account Service strategically places roadblocks along the path to trip them up. They feel the AE just doesn't know a good idea. In some cases they may be right, but in my experience I have found (with a few exceptions) AEs provide the analytical thinking and organizational skills that many creatives lack. As creative lead, you must set the standard. The Account Service team is not placed in the agency to keep you from doing great work. They are there to ensure that you and your team provide work that remains true to the brand, relevant to the consumer, and strategically sound.

Cooperating with the AEs does not mean you are settling for bland creative ideas. When you meet with your AE, ask as many questions as needed to tease out the information you'll need to do the job. What can you ask to get the details you need?

- What does this client like?

- What does this client not want to see in a creative solution?

- Is there any reference material that can guide you to a solution?

Getting answers to your questions can result in useful facts such as, *"By the way, the client really likes monkeys and hates using testimonials."* Now that you have some parameters, you can use monkeys and make sure you don't use testimonials. Win-win.

A good way to keep your AEs on your side and understanding the direction your team's creatives are progressing is by keeping them in the loop. When you have ideas, share them. Get them onboard. You can walk them through your thinking process, the research that led to the creative direction, and any insights that have helped form the concepts. The best AEs will trust you as the creative leader and will not overstep their boundaries and try to give you their opinions. Any comments they have will be based on the strategy that has been outlined for the client.

Once it's time to present to the client, give the AE a preview and let her know what you feel is a "must-have" element and what can be "sacrificed" to the conceptual graveyard. By giving her tips like this, you will arm her with the ammunition needed to defend your concepts, if need be.

Once you get to the production portion of the gig, be sure to notify the AE of any changes, revisions, or delays during this phase. If it incurs additional cost or time, your AE needs to inform the client.

Your AEs will communicate quite a bit with the client. You can depend on them to deal with a lot of the things you simply don't want to deal with. They are liaisons between you and your client. Their actions can remove some of the stress that comes along with being a creative lead.

All sunshine and butterflies, right? Sure. There will be disagreements and AEs that you either don't get along with or just don't like. Well, suck it up. You are the creative leader. Your job is to provide the client with creative solutions to their marketing challenges. Where you lead, your creative team will follow. If you speak poorly about the AEs in Account Service, your creative team will do the same. If you grunt and grumble when an AE tells you some of the concepts don't work, your creative team will do the same. On the contrary, if you treat your AEs as valuable members of the creative process, your creative team will do the same.

You can do it. Make it work and it'll make your life easier.

# Disseminating The Message With The Media Department

The media department buys the advertising time and space required for a successful advertising campaign. This field of influence includes TV, radio time, Out-of-Home (billboards, posters, guerrilla), magazine and newspaper insertions, web banners… pretty much anywhere that an ad can be placed for a fee (or even for free). To do their job effectively, your media team needs to work closely with the creative team.

As a creative lead, you cannot work in a vacuum. You can't simply come up with ideas and expect them to be executed. You need to understand what the client's advertising budget is and work with media to understand what you can and can't afford before you start coming up with your audacious ideas.

Once you determine what type of exposure your client wants, you can work with your media team to see what is feasible. Remember, it does no good to come up with a fantastic idea that ends up being seen only once because it was so expensive to execute and get out to the public.

# Getting The Word Out With Public Relations

Your public relations team promotes the agency via editorial coverage. They will do so via "earned" or "free" media—stories appearing on websites, newspapers, magazines, and TV programs—as compared to "paid media" or advertisements that are secured through your media buying team.

Your public relations teammates are experts at anticipating, analyzing, and interpreting public opinion, attitudes, and issues that might impact what the general public thinks about your client. They will

- write and distribute press releases and speeches
- send pitches to journalists to try and get them interested in a particular angle so they'll write a story on your client
- create and execute special events designed for public outreach and media relations
- conduct market research on your client's messaging
- develop crisis relations strategies
- handle social media promotions and responses

A great PR person is a good listener of the marketplace and will know what conversation starters will not only work, but also what might catch fire and get your clients lots of good publicity. You can always look to your public relations team to help you come up with some out-of-the-box *(seriously overused term)* thinking. They can either give you a direction to follow or sometimes they will provide the nugget of information that gets you started and can lead to a great guerrilla campaign.

Give them your time and listen to their ideas. Keep in mind, everyone can be creative, not just the people who work in your department.

## In a Nutshell

Think of the advertising creative team as a group of intermediaries. These are the individuals who try to link a company's brand to their target and create desire. The key to remember as a creative leader is that you are not the only people who influence what a brand has to say or how it looks. You are one part of the equation.

Other parts of the equation include your traffic manager, who keeps the jobs flowing smoothly through the department; the AE, who is the liaison between the client and the agency; the media department, which negotiates all the promotional buys; public relations, which can get the message out through various publicity channels; the accounts team, which bills the clients and makes sure the magic paycheck fairy visits your bank account twice a month; and of course the executives who started the agency and keep it moving.

As a CD, you will lead your creative team, but you will be involved with all of the other departments and individuals who help take a branding campaign from a simple scribble or thought to fruition. They will look to you for your insight, experience, and creative acumen. Be the conductor and help all the elements of your agency orchestra to work in harmony.

# Leading a Design Creative Team

## Fighting the war against visual corruption

Running a design team in a studio is similar to running an advertising agency creative team with several exceptions. For large studios, you will most likely have account executives to act as a buffer between the creatives and clients. At small studios, chances are the creatives deal directly with clients. In both configurations, you will still be leading your team to ideate and produce work that solves communication challenges that your client is experiencing. However, there is a difference. While an ad agency creative team is addressing communications challenges with solutions that include TV or radio spots, out-of-home tactics, and print campaigns, design studios deal with visual challenges in ways that require visual solutions in the form of identities, environmental design, package design, websites, and so on.

© Eleazar Hernández 2017
E. Hernández, *Leading Creative Teams*, DOI 10.1007/978-1-4842-2056-6_4

Because graphic design is so inclusive with regards to what types of solutions it can provide, it addresses visual challenges in a number of different areas including

- Advertising design
- Architectural signage and environmental design
- Books and publication design
- Visual identity systems
- Film, video, and digital graphics
- Packaging and point-of-purchase design
- Social, cultural, and political communications

Each of these areas is a specialized type of communication design focusing on different client needs. Design studios can specialize in one of these specific areas or they can be generalists that don't limit themselves to a particular niche, but work with many types of clients and touch many different types of projects.

To be successful in a design environment, as the creative lead you must ensure that your team is producing visually compelling work that addresses the elements and principles of design to solve client challenges. The key here is to understand that as designers we do not simply create work based on whims or the zeitgeist of the moment; elements and principles must be utilized in smart ways along with messaging to engage with your client's audience. To lead a creative team successfully, you must understand these fundamentals of good design.

# Elements of Graphic Design

Graphic design focuses on the aesthetics of an assignment by strategically implementing elements together to visually address client challenges. While some may argue this point, I believe a successful graphic design solution should address a marketing challenge, not obscure it. In other words, a design should not be so visually distracting that it takes away from the content or function of the messaging. Instead, it should enhance the message by inviting recipients or users to build trust and interest in the client's brand. The elements of graphic design are as follows:

- **Line:** A mark made by a tool as it is drawn across a surface (open path). A line's type or attributes refer to the way it moves from its beginning to its end. Line quality refers to how the line is drawn.
- **Shape:** A closed form or a closed path.

- **Color**: The elements of color can be divided into three categories: *Hue*, which is the name of the color; *Value*, which is the range of lightness or darkness (shade, tone, and tint); and *Saturation*, which is the brightness or dullness of a color.

- **Texture**: The tactile quality of a surface or the representation of such a surface quality.

- **Format**: Brochures, posters, business cards, book covers, shopping bags, envelopes, newsletters, magazines, and newspapers are just some of the many formats designers use. Whether it is a page or a business card, whatever you start out with is the format.

# Principles of Graphic Design

Where the elements of graphic design are the components that make up any design solution, the principles of design outline how those elements can be utilized. They govern how your creative team can create relationships between the elements in a design and organize the composition as a whole. Successful graphic design incorporates the use of the principles to communicate the intended message effectively. The principles are as follows:

- **Balance**: The equal distribution of weight. There are two basic approaches to the arrangement of elements in design: *Symmetry* is the arrangement of all identical or similar visual elements so they are visually distributed on either side of an imaginary axis. *Asymmetry* is the arrangement of dissimilar or unequal elements along the page. To achieve asymmetrical balance, the position, visual weight, size, value, color, shape, and texture of a mark on the page must be considered and weighed against every other mark.

- **Emphasis**: The idea that some things are more important than others.

- **Visual hierarchy**: Arrangement of elements according to emphasis.

- **Rhythm**: A pattern that is created by repeating or varying elements with consideration given to the space between them, and by establishing a sense of movement from one element to another.

- **Unity**: The relationship among the elements of a design that helps relay an overall sense of cohesiveness. Unity allows the viewer to see an integrated whole rather than unrelated parts.

- **Illusion of 3D space**: The illusion of spatial depth where some objects seem closer to the viewer than others. Three ways to create illusion are scale, volume, and perspective. *Scale* is the size of one shape or object in comparison to another, and when used effectively it can make elements appear to project forward or recede on the page. *Volume* is the illusion of a form with mass and weight (a shape with a back as well as a front). *Perspective* is the idea that diagonals moving toward a point on the horizon will imitate the recession of space into the distance and create the illusion of spatial depth.

The elements and principles of graphic design inform how we create, but we can't rely solely on them to be successful leaders. As creative leads in the design field we must provide our clients with more than aesthetics. We must also provide strategic insight to our offerings when clients request our services.

# Design and Strategy

Whether you currently hold the position of creative director or you are a senior-level designer striving to move forward in your career, you must be prepared to address different solutions when working with your clients. Some clients will come to you with a solution already in mind that they simply want your team to execute. Others will come with a challenge in mind, but no solution. Still others will come with a challenge and a solution. To be successful, you must always strive to consider solutions strategically.

You must provide your clients with strategic insights at the beginning of the project before they get too far into the creative process. If a client comes to you with a tactical request to simply create a communications vehicle (brochure, direct mail campaign, billboards, posters, etc.), ask questions. Find out why they want this item created. What is the strategic rationale behind the request? The best way to address tactical requests is to work with your clients as partners. You must be more than vendors.

You should strive to be trusted partners who can be counted on to provide great service, honest feedback, and strategic advice. Take a genuine interest in their business. Read articles related to their industry, proactively research competitors, talk to them about their operations and strategy. By remaining informed, you may be able to anticipate any new requests and challenges. Some of the most successful design firms have embraced strategy as an important aspect of the services they provide. As a result, they have been able to successfully address client concerns and streamline their creative process while being able to honestly advise their clients.

With the advent of subscription-based software such as Adobe Creative Cloud, along with the increasing skills among in-house employees, studios may find their value decreasing among clients. To combat this you need to increase your value as a strategic partner. How many times do you want to hear that a client has hired an internal designer to provide the services that you provide? What then? If you are a strategic partner, they rely on you not only for your designs, but also for your strategic advice and insight.

# Working with a Design Team

Have you ever witnessed or been part of a team that works together really well? Team members bounce ideas off of each other, without any apparent jealousy or duplicity. The group runs like a well-oiled machine. Sure, there might be disagreements, but the great thing about them is that they get past the speed bumps and continue to work as a team. If you have the opportunity to work with a team like that, consider yourself fortunate. On the flipside, you may end up on a design team where egos, jealousy, and poor attitudes rule the day. Regardless of the type of team dynamic you walk in to, your task is to lead them.

Building, leading, and guiding a team are difficult. You want to get your hands dirty and keep being intimately involved in the design work. However, as previously mentioned you must step back and be a creative leader, not necessarily a creative doer. To do so requires that you develop your design team's abilities. You must judge when your design teams needs you to be involved in the assignments, and if they do, to what extent. Some projects simply require you to provide air cover, while others need you to be involved every step of the way.

# Guarding Your Team's Creative Flow

One of the most difficult things you will do is try to keep your team focused on their main design tasks and not distracted by other miscellaneous "quick jobs" that float in to the department. By "quick jobs" I mean those jobs that come in and disrupt the flow of your team. It's very easy for smaller jobs to pull your team from the task at hand and distract them from what they are currently working on. Every time they are pulled away from their work, they will have to take time to refocus and get back into the right frame of mind to continue. Sometimes disruptions are unavoidable and relatively easy to knock out. Many times, the "quick jobs" come in because of a lack of communication or planning on either the client side or the account service side. Even worse, it comes from a lack of understanding regarding how long jobs take to be accomplished. Both problems are easily remedied.

Whether you use an online system like Advantage or ProWorkFlow or you have a simpler traffic system, be sure that anyone requesting work consistently places any and all jobs into the system. You may be accused of not being collaborative, but in reality you are. By ensuring that people put work through the system, you can ensure that all jobs are given the proper amount of attention. This will, in turn, minimize any potential issues with jobs being turned too quickly and risking their overall quality. If a job isn't on this list of projects then it's not getting done. No ifs, ands, or buts about it. You need to run a tight ship in order to keep your team on track. Unnecessary distractions can be a huge problem if they are allowed to impact the team's overall deliverables schedule and the quality of the work that leaves the studio.

# Design Process

Graphic design is an active process. Your design team will be filled with designers who are creative problem solvers. Working within time constraints and established budgets, designers employ universal design principles as a means to generate effective communications solutions. In responding to the challenges posed by each project, your designers will have to use a combination of their imaginative and analytical skills. To accomplish this, your team should follow a defined process to ensure that they can effectively address client challenges.

A good working process includes steps to ensure strong client communication, creative execution, and proactive management throughout the duration of a project. The most effective process ensures that you can deliver creative work to your clients accurately. Figure 4-1 illustrates the six-phase design process that has been applicable to most of the projects I have led. It has taken a while for me to generate this process, and I will outline each phase in detail in the sections that follow.

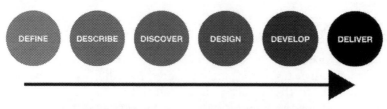

**Figure 4-1.** Design process

# Define

The first phase of the process is all about setting parameters for the work that will follow. Starting the relationship with clear communication at this stage will save you time, money, and headaches later on. The three key steps are as follows:

- ***Initial Client Conversation***: This is the initial meeting and schmoozing stage. Potential clients may come to your attention in a variety of ways, including community or business events, requests for proposal (RFP) and referrals, and so on.

- ***Establishment of Initial Scope***: Determine what the project will entail. Be clear about the initial scope so that you can avoid any scope creep later in the game. Scope creep—when a client expands the number and/or type of deliverables needed for a job—ripples difficulties throughout the process. Imagine the client has approved a budget for a logo design, but after everything is moving forward they request an identity system as well. Save your budget and your sanity by being clear at the start.

- ***Preliminary Estimate***: Think through what has been asked of you and your team. Work with production to develop an accurate estimate. Be sure to itemize the document so the client can see where the majority of the work will be done.

# Describe

This phase is all about the ***proposal submission***. Write up a proposal that includes the elements that you defined as necessities for their job. Once complete, submit the document to the client.

# Discover

The third phase is all about asking questions and doing research to learn as much as you can about the client, the product, and the objectives of both. Specifically, ask

- ***Who Is the Client?*** This is your opportunity to learn who you are designing for. What is their unique selling proposition? What have they done in the past? Are they leaders in their field or are they trying to be?

- **Who Is the Audience?** Who will you be speaking to? What do they like? What do they hate? What are they doing? You will need to understand the demographics of your target to be able to speak to them appropriately.

- **What Is the Operating Space?** Where will you be designing? Is it the digital realm? Is it print? What kind of print? Posters? Marketing collateral? Out-of-home?

- **What Is the Product/Service?** What are they selling? Would you use it? Do you believe in it?

- **What Are the Objectives?** What are they trying to accomplish this project? Is what they have asked you to design the right way to solve their challenge? Should they rethink it?

# Design

The Design phase is where many creative directors get confused. They tend to get so excited about the job that they jump to this phase prematurely. When you jump to brainstorming and designing before going through the Define, Describe, and Discover phases, you risk being off-target. This results in having to do the work again, which then means you will go over budget. If you begin with the previous phases to set the stage, this phase is where all the fun begins.

- **Brainstorming**: This is where the fun starts. It's time for you to motivate your creative team to get started with design ideas. Check out Chapter 5 for tips and tricks.

- **Vehicle Establishment (print/broadcast/interactive, etc.)**: Where you will place your work will determine how you design it. Find out.

- **Initial Vendor Involvement**: Who will be producing your work? If it's print, for instance, who can do what you require for the job?

- **Preliminary Design**: After brainstorming you'll want to create some very loose comps for your client to review.

- **Initial Client Presentation**: It's show time. This is where you get to present your solutions to your client. You will either win or lose based on your presentation skills. Be sure to get familiar with Chapter 8.

- **Review and Refinement**: Time to make edits based on client feedback. No matter what you're working on or how perfect everything looks, there will almost always be client edits. Get the work to your client as soon as possible so they can provide feedback and get it back to you.

- **Design Finalized**: You've received the final edits. Make them, and get client final approval for the job to go to press. Never send a job to the printer without your client's signed or e-mailed approval.

# Develop

You're almost there. Your team's files are complete and it's time to move on to production. This phase is about working with vendors to put your ideas into their final format. The two main tasks are

- **Deliverable Development**: Your designs will be checked for their printability. As you probably know, the printer you are using typically has someone on staff that pre-flights your files to ensure that everything is set correctly. If your file is not absolutely perfect, they will contact you and let you know. If for some reason, a problem makes it past the prepress check, you will run into problems during the printing process. That said, I don't like to leave my potential success in the hands of others. I believe it's in your best interest to create a checklist of necessary links and settings for each file so you can have your team conduct a final check before sending files to your vendor. Better safe than sorry.

- **Vendor Coordination**: Your traffic/production manager (if you have one) will take care of this stage. You provide the press-ready files and they coordinate with the printer/vendor who will produce your work.

# Deliver

**Everyone smiles** as the client takes delivery. This is the best part of the job because it's where all of your hard work pays off. Be sure to keep copies of your work to use for awards submissions and your portfolio.

# Know Your Design Team

Designers are an interesting breed. We get excited about paper, varnish, colors, and pretty much anything visually exciting. We enjoy touching, feeling, and yes, even smelling things whether it's the latest paper promotion, a new book, a beautifully designed direct mail campaign… yup, pretty much everything. Through our eccentricities our ideas flow.

Some of us are collectors of random things (BTW, they are action figures not toys!) while others are minimalists. Some like loud music while others like it to be quiet. First and foremost, designers are observers and lovers of beautiful and useful objects, messages, and experiences.

Good designers tend to pay attention to everything in their environment as they progress through their day to gain insight and inspiration from the world around. They make connections and ask questions about how objects and messages work, if they are strategically sound, what they are, how things look, and what they mean.

Designers have a desire to create things that inspire them and then share them with their teammates, their clients… the world. It's the observations they make that lead them to design things that had not previously existed, to push beyond the expected and deliver work that is not only functional, but beautifully informed by their curiosity. This curiosity is at the core of the designer, and doesn't always make sense to everyone else.

How do you work with this band of crazies? How do you control or direct this unique, versatile, insightful, driven, visually curious band of creatives who don't typically like to be forced within a box or rule or made to work in an overly corporate environment?

The better you know your team, the more you will realize that you are dealing with a juxtaposition of interesting traits. Designers are introverted enough to want to dive deep into a project. They become consumed by details, fonts, colors, texture. They are also extroverted enough to read people and address the needs and desires of a client to shape the experience of their target audiences. Interesting people, your design team, very interesting, as you may already know—or will soon find out.

Hopefully this description of your design team hasn't made you believe that they/we are a bunch of weirdos. Designers are more than just people who hate dress codes and like to wear sneakers to work. We are creative and complex people who don't like to follow trends. We like to discover and start trends. Our constant observations of our surroundings help inform our desire to make the world a better place. A better designed place.

Well, at least that's what all the voices in my head tell me.

# In a Nutshell

If you take anything away from this chapter, it is that you must understand the individuals who make up your design team, your design clients, and your design product. Your design team will address client issues in terms of the visual challenges presented to them. You must determine when to guide them and when to step back and allow them to flourish. Lead your team in a way that not only challenges them, but allows them to feel as if they are working in an environment that appreciates bold leaps and rewards innovative thinking.

The somewhat odd part of this chapter is that I addressed the elements and principles of design. While it may have seemed as if you were going through Graphic Design 101, I believe it's important to remember these standards because they are significant part of everything we do.

I have also provided an overview of the design process. While it may not always be possible to do so, if you are able to work in a systematic way, you can alleviate stress and keep order while empowering your team to do their best work. Your team will be filled with different personalities, levels of experience, and temperaments. You must strive to encourage your team to do their best at all times. Nurture their individuality without sacrificing the process that will ensure that jobs are completed in a timely manner and at or under budget.

Above all, have fun. In a design environment you have the opportunity to lead a creative team which aspires to ideate, develop, and produce great things. Nurture their creativity. Guide their exuberance. Cheer for their innovation. Celebrate their success. Then prepare for the next challenge.

# Brainstorming

## Where do all those crazy ideas come from?

You've got the creative brief that outlines the parameters of the job. You've done some preliminary research to help wrap your head around your assignment, and you've checked out what other people have done on the subject. Now after all of this information gathering, you've got lots of random thoughts and ideas rolling around in your head. Slowly, your brain begins to make connections. You're out getting your 3:00 p.m. wake-me-up coffee and the shape of the foam on your skinny vanilla latte inspires a visual treatment. You're eating lunch with coworkers at a local bistro and hear a song that makes you think of headlines. The initial information has been processed in your mind and is being transformed into different forms. Images begin to form. Words and messaging come together. It's time to brainstorm.

Brainstorming: A ubiquitous word that is used by so many different people, that it feels as if it has been part of the process of creative thinking since the beginning of time—and from the standpoint of advertising, maybe it has. In reality, it hasn't been around that long. In 1942, Alex Faickney Osborn, one of the founders of BBDO published a book titled How to "Think Up"[1] in which he presented the technique of brainstorming—something that was being uniquely used at BBDO as part of their ideation process. The term "brainstorm" was popularized by Osborn in 1953 book Applied Imagination: Principles and Procedures of Creative Problem Solving.[2] Maybe other agencies were "brainstorming" but using

---

[1] Alex Faickney Osborn. How to "Think Up" (New York, London: McGraw-Hill Book Co., 1942).
[2] Alex Faickney Osborn. Applied Imagination: Principles and Procedures of Creative Problem Solving (New York: Charles Scribner's Sons, 1953).

© Eleazar Hernández 2017
E. Hernández, Leading Creative Teams, DOI 10.1007/978-1-4842-2056-6_5

a different term to describe their ideation process, maybe they weren't. Since Osborn was the first to publicize the technique, he gets the credit for its creation. Now brainstorming is done in virtually all industries when individuals or groups are trying to come up with creative solutions to problems.

Brainstorming is a creativity exercise in which individuals or groups of people gather together to generate a list of ideas spontaneously and in rapid succession with the goal of trying to find solutions to a specific problem. Many believe—as do I—that brainstorming is a skill that can be developed. To be successful, you must be prepared to throw out ideas that may or may not be fully formed and be willing to risk criticism and rejection. You can work alone or in a group. Brainstorming can be done in a day or it could take several days. The bottom line is you need to be able to generate ideas and allow them to bloom into something viable.

Now the fun begins.

# Capturing Ideas

Whether you decide to go the old-fashioned route with a notepad or sketchbook or go digital with a program like Evernote, it is very important that you keep a record of your ideas, whether it's in the form of scribbles or written notes. There are a number of reasons to keep your brainstorm notes.

First, keeping a record is a great way to see how you evolve as a creative thinker. When you go back to older books, you can see how your thought process has changed over time. Second, it provides a place that you can refer to when you need a creative boost. I have found that sometimes going back through my old books can help spark a new idea. Third, you can use your notes and sketches as a way to get everything out of your head. Sometimes writing things down and getting them out of your head is a way to clear the path for newer, better ideas. There are any number of reasons that you should keep a book of your brainstorming. I have a stack of hardbound sketchbooks from years of scribbles and brainstorming. Once you determine you want to keep track of your sketches and brainstorm, there are several ways to keep your notes safe and orderly: sketchbooks, project folders, and project binders.

## Sketchbook

The sketchbook is the perfect place to put all of your ideas and inspiration. This is my absolute "go-to" method of recording. I recommend you carry a sketchbook at all times. It should be attached to you like a tattoo on your skin.

Sketchbooks come in various sizes—from small books that fit in your pocket to large 11×17-inch books. When considering sketchbooks, there are various brands, sizes, styles, covers, and paper stocks for you to choose. As a matter of fact, there are even several subscription-based sketchbook programs available that will deliver a new sketchbook right to your doorstep every month. You simply need to select the one that works best for you.

Once you've selected a book, it may take you some time to get used to carrying and using it. Until it becomes a habit, it's very easy to forget. It may feel like it's just one more thing that you'll have to carry around with you to work, home, the grocery store, the movies, on dates (Ok, maybe not on dates. I'll give you a break on that one.), pretty much everywhere you go. You should strive to carry your sketchbook with you as much as possible because—like it or not—you can't plan when you will be hit by inspiration. Sometimes ideas won't come to you during a scheduled time or there will be times that you start ideating with a blank piece of paper and end with a blank piece of paper.

Your sketchbook is your safe place. Write down everything. Draw in it, develop thumbnail sketches, take notes, make a shopping list, doodle during your meetings (Figure 5-1). Tape reference material from magazines or other printed materials on the pages. Don't worry about what it looks like. You aren't creating a sketchbook for anyone's approval. You don't ever have to show the pages to anyone. It's yours and yours alone.

**Figure 5-1.** No matter which writing utensil you use, get your ideas down in a sketchbook.

## Project Folder

If you don't want to always carry around a sketchbook (shame on you), that's fine. The next best thing you can do is create a project folder for all of your projects or clients. This can be a dump folder where you place all your meeting notes, scribbles, or random ephemera that you collect for inspiration.

If this is the route you choose, get in the habit of collecting things that inspire you and saving them so you can add them to the folder and have access to them when you are ready to begin brainstorming.

# Project Binder

Something that works for larger projects is a project binder. The binder helps you keep large amounts of information organized. Honestly, I have never tried this technique (I'm more of a Moleskine or sketchbook guy), but workmates of mine swear by it. They use a three-ring binder to hold any materials that are considered relevant to the project. From scribbles and notes to e-mails and vendor invoices, the project binder becomes the ultimate holder of project or client information. For items too small or large to punch holes in, try dropping them into acetate sleeves that drop into the binder for safe keeping. Because the binder will get very large, you will need to organize it in a coherent manner so you can refer to it in the future.

Utilizing tabs and breaking the binder up into sections is a great way to organize it. You can start with a section that contains the creative brief and any notes that you jotted down during the meetings that initiated the project. The next section could be filled with images for your reference. From images grabbed from websites to copies or scans of books and magazines, this section can be filled with all of the items that will spark your imagination. A third section could be filled with all of the scribbles (thumbnail sketches) that you create to work through your process. The fourth section can hold all of the mock-ups that you create. Initial logos, brochure comps, billboard mock-ups, or TV storyboards can fill this section. There could be a fifth and final section that holds the final, approved creative. This last section is the icing on the cake: something you can use when you are working with junior staffers to show them how to work through the creative process.

# Ground Rules

Before I go into detail about brainstorming, let's go over a few ground rules for both the leader of the brainstorm session and the participants. If these are followed, the brainstorm will be both easier to get started and more enjoyable for everyone. Remember, nobody likes to brainstorm in a room full of crickets.

# Rule 1—Inspired Location

If at all possible, avoid holding brainstorming sessions in locations that lack personality and comfort. You and your team will only be inspired when you feel comfortable and nourished. Several characteristics of a creative location are as follows:

- It's fun, comfortable, physically enjoyable, and stimulating.
- It's a safe environment for the team to throw out ideas.
- It's well lit.
- It's not overly distracting.

If you happen to work in an environment that has all of these characteristics, fantastic! If not, try to find locations where you and your creative team can hold frequent brainstorm sessions. Find a place that inspires creativity. I have held brainstorms in local coffee shops, on the lawn at a museum, in the gallery of a museum, or even while walking around downtown San Antonio. It doesn't matter where. The only thing that matters is that you are in a safe place that gets your people talking and sharing ideas.

Why is it important to have a safe place to brainstorm? Anyone who has achieved success as a creative leader will say that their success hinged on self-confidence and no fear of failure.[3] Because they felt they could work confidently, they were comfortable taking risks. Their risk taking is the fundamental reason their work stands out. How can you help your creative team feel as if they have a safe place for creativity in which they are free to take risks without fear of failure? One good way is to refer to ground rule number 2.

# Rule 2—No No's

The first and most important rule is NEVER SAY NO. The word "no" has power: the power to stop all creative thinking and make someone retreat and stop participating. The word "no" can lead to concept mediocrity. There is nothing more frustrating to a creative than to be working through an idea and have someone chime in with a, "No, I've seen that before" or "No, that won't work." Rather than say "no" you should strive to be positive and add to an idea, not take away from it.

Instead of saying "no" try "Yes, and." "Yes, and" is a way for you to add to an idea that was tossed out during the brainstorm. This not only supports the person who put the idea on the table, but it allows you to expand it. A simple "yes, and" will keep the energy going and will lead to other ideas.

# Rule 3—Be Prepared

It is both annoying and very disrespectful to show up for a brainstorm session unprepared. Your lack of preparation signals to the team that you do not feel the client or team is important enough to spend your time understanding the

---

[3]Mark Oldach. *Creativity for Graphic Designers* (Cincinnati: North Light Books, Inc., 1995), p. 61.

marketing challenges. In addition, your lack of preparation will set the stage for your creative team to follow. If you habitually show up for brainstorm sessions unprepared, it's only a matter of time before they soon follow suit.

## Rule 4—Time Limit

Believe it or not, brainstorming takes energy. If you try to brainstorm for too long, you will lose focus and just waste time. You can feel out your team and gain a pretty good understanding of how long they can last in a brainstorm session and adjust your sessions accordingly. I have found that one hour seems to be a good length of time before breaking up. You can do multiple brainstorm sessions throughout the day if need be. Just break them up to give people time to compose their thoughts. You can also continue to brainstorm the next day. A great creative team will continue to think through the assignment even if it's not at the forefront of their minds.

# Brainstorming Solo

There will be times you will need to come up with ideas on your own. When you brainstorm alone, no matter which directions your mind heads, you will only go in a direction that is determined by your experience, knowledge, likes, dislikes, and so on. Don't stress too much. Brainstorming alone is not impossible. It's done all the time. However, because you have to select only the best ideas from your own mind, you will have to be disciplined. Don't fall in love with any particular ideas because you may be the only one that understands them. Know that once you open yourself up and present your ideas to internal staff and clients, some of the ideas may rise to the surface and shine brightly while others will die in a big ball of flames on the conference room table.

# Brainstorming In a Group

If two heads are better than one and four heads are better than two, then brainstorming in a group is obviously the ideal situation for coming up with a greater number of ideas. There can never be too many *participating* minds in a brainstorm. The key word here is *participating*. The best brainstorm sessions will occur when several people get together with their minds open and ready to go. Verbalizing ideas in a group is the best way to take ideas beyond what is possible alone. Simply having bodies in chairs does not make for a good brainstorming session. Each individual should actively participate and contribute to the process. Everyone brings something different to the session. Capitalize on that and you will soon be developing great ideas.

If you're going to brainstorm in a group, as the creative lead, you must be sure to keep the ball rolling, pick up steam when the talking slows down, and keep the energy going to facilitate great ideas. Brainstorming is an art. Mark Oldach outlines several tips to keep in mind when brainstorming in a group[4]:

- Everyone is equal.

- Be respectful.

- During a brainstorm there are no bad ideas.

- No judgment or evaluation of ideas.

- Record everything. All thoughts, statements, and ideas.

- Start with a review of the problem.

- Restate the problem in your own words.

- List words that relate to the challenge as a means to discover and explore possible pathways.

- Silence during the brainstorm is bad, energetic chatter is good.

- Everyone must participate. Don't allow anyone to dominate the session. If someone doesn't participate, call on them. Ask their opinions.

- Assign a facilitator and time keeper. They are not the leader or evaluator or the one with the ideas.

- Brainstorm when everyone is fresh. Avoid first thing in the morning and late in the afternoon.

- Avoid interruptions. Put your phones on silent or better yet, leave them at your desk. Unless there is a genuine emergency that requires immediate attention, *do not* interrupt the session for any reason

- Keep the brainstorm light and playful. If the room lacks fun and laughter, chances are the ideas will be dull, uninspired, and predictable.

Brainstorming in groups is one of the most difficult ways to come up with ideas. Invariably there are people who will shine and dominate the session, but there will also be those who shrink back and don't really say much. Throwing out ideas is difficult because our ideas are those little nuggets of ourselves that we are tossing out to everyone to get judged. They can rise and save the world

---

[4]Mark Oldach. *Creativity for Graphic Designers* (Cincinnati: North Light Books, Inc., 1995), pp. 60–61.

or they can die a horrible little death right before our eyes. As the creative lead, you must strive to get everyone engaged and keep them participating. You want to make sure that brainstorms are a positive experience for everyone. When they are fun, when people are laughing and having a good time, when your team is throwing out good ideas that are informed by the initial research they conducted, you'll be amazed at the kind of concepts that appear.

# Parameters

Although it may seem like something great, having a project without parameters can be difficult to deal with. Imagine if you were given an assignment to paint the sky. What part would you paint? Would you paint sunrise or sunset? Would it be sunny or cloudy? Are there any jets in the sky? How about birds? Are we looking up to the sky or are we flying in the sky? The questions can be endless. As creatives, we complain about restrictions, and want more room to be creative. We love the idea of pushing beyond restraints and rules. However, that is not realistic. We need parameters to help guide our creativity

When you're presented with a client challenge, strive to truly understand the project parameters. When the client has objectives, figure out how to attain them. Understand who the client's intended audience is and what they like. Examine their needs and prepare to answer them.

# No Idea Is Bad

In the beginning stages of your brainstorming, it's important to keep the ideas flowing—good, bad, boring, hot, or cold. Remember, during a brainstorming session your goal is to produce as many ideas as you can.

Be free with your thoughts. Let them come. Don't get stuck developing one thought or direction, or you risk generating a limited supply of ideas. If you and your team mix, refine, and evolve as many ideas as possible, you can generate a virtually endless supply of solutions that can be reviewed against the client's criteria during the editing phase.

Once you feel you have an adequate amount, have reached the time limit, or feel everyone is too drained to continue, gather the ideas and take a break.

---

▓ **Warning** During the brainstorm, don't stop at the first idea just because it seems to be perfect for the client. For that matter don't stop at the second, third, or even the thirtieth. You never know what's going to emerge from the ashes. Your next idea might be the most creative one. You should continue thinking about the project even after the brainstorm session has ended, even if it's in the back of your mind while you are working on other projects.

---

# Empty Your Brain of the Obvious

When you sit down to brainstorm, the first ideas you come up with are usually the obvious ones. Those solutions are usually the culmination of information you've collected and influences you've unknowingly absorbed from television, magazines, websites, and so on. Although the ideas you come up with may be good, they will probably not be unique. As a matter of fact, the first thoughts you have are most likely also the first thought many other creatives may have. Empty your brain of the ideas that come first and move on to better ones that are uniquely you.

# The Path of Most Resistance

As you brainstorm, your ideas will begin to take you down different paths that may be difficult to follow. It's easy to travel down the easiest path—the one that is full of ideas that you've seen before. Ideas other creatives have already put out into the world. To create something truly different and impactful, you must strive to go where others haven't gone.

You are unique. You have experiences and ways of thinking that no other creative has. To stand out from the crowd, utilize what is unique about yourself. Make the connections only you can with the information you have gathered.

# Understand Yourself

The more you brainstorm, the more you will begin to understand the way your mind works through problems. Different people process information differently. Learn what gets your imagination going and what works best for you. Some people do their best work in the morning, some are night owls. Some need complete silence, while others do better with loud music playing. Everyone is different.

It's frustrating when you're trying to brainstorm and your mind just isn't in it. No matter what you do the ideas just don't come. Once you figure out what works best for you, you can be better prepared to capture ideas when they most often come to you.

# Combine Different Parts into a New Whole

Some of the best ideas will come from your mind making unexpected connections. The only way to do this is to have lots of information from which to pull. Try getting into the habit of approaching assignments from different perspectives. Sometimes we get so caught up in the work that we forget that there are many perspectives that we can use to examine problems.

When you begin developing concepts, try ideating from the opposite perspective. If something is white, make it black. If something is usually done with lots of photos, try white space. If something is small, make it huge. Even if you don't decide to pursue a different perspective, exploring can at least spark more ideas.

# Know When to Walk Away

You've obtained the client brief. You've researched the target audience. You explored the advertising landscape. Now you sit, ready to begin brainstorming. Words, images, colors: all swirl in your head. You're ready for the ideas to start flowing. Here they come… and… nothing. What the hell?!

You know you have a grip on what needs to be done, but all your thoughts mean nothing. You keep trying to develop concepts and nothing seems to stick. Soon you get distracted. You begin to do other things. You check e-mail. You jump onto Facebook or Instagram. You start to organize your desk or walk around the office and chat with friends or coworkers. You've hit the wall. The harder you try to come up with an idea, the more frustrated you become.

This situation isn't unique. It happens to everyone on occasion, and everyone deals with it in their own way. Recognize when you've hit a creative roadblock and walk away. It doesn't matter if the deadline is tomorrow. If you continue to try and force creativity, one of two things will happen:

1. You won't come up with an idea; or

2. You will come up with a lame idea that is neither creative nor original.

Problems such as number 2 above happen more frequently than we'd like them to. What really sucks about this is when you present the idea to the client and they like it. They give you the green light to proceed, and you're stuck working on a project that pretty much sucked from the beginning. As you suffer through it, you will lack pride and passion. As much as I hate to admit it, I have experienced this one personally. It really REALLY sucks!

Part of working through creative blocks is understanding when you do your best work. I find that I usually have my best ideas first thing in the morning after a good workout. I have tried all-nighters. They don't work for me. I usually go through what I call the "*Stages of Uninspired Creative Emotions.*"

- Stage One (7:00 p.m.): Resignation I—Now I've got everything. Time to get to work.

- Stage Two (11:00 p.m.): Euphoria—I've got this. I'll be done in no time! I love designing!

- Stage Three (2:00 a.m.): Anger—What the hell is this client thinking about when they asked us for this? Why am I the only one up working?! I bet everyone else is asleep! I hate design! I'm gonna go back to college and get a degree in a job that ends at 5:00 p.m.!

- Stage Four (3:00 a.m.): Bargaining—I swear, if I can just get through this, I promise I will never over-research again. I know I said this last time, but this time I mean it! Really mean it!

- Stage Five (5:00 a.m.): Resignation II—Ok, I've finally have an idea. This is gonna have to work because I'm running out of time.

- Stage Six (8:00 a.m.): Clean-up—Time to shower. What is that smell?! This is as good as the project is gonna get. Move along. Nothing to see here. Today is really gonna suck.

- Stage Seven (10:00 a.m.): What?!—The client has rescheduled the meeting?! I have another day to work on this?! What the F@#$!

First, you really want to avoid trying to push through creative blocks at night. Contrary to popular belief, all-nighters are not fun. Especially when you're working alone. In my experience, I have found that getting some sleep and starting fresh is the best way for me to cure any creative blocks I need to get past. 'nuff said.

# Editing and Evaluating Ideas

First, don't edit brainstorm sessions until they are over. Having good judgment and being able to evaluate and pick out good ideas from bad ones are the hallmarks of a great creative leader. However, editing has no place during the actual brainstorm session. Remember, you are there to encourage your team to shoot out lots of ideas. Judgment stifles creative thinking.

Second, using realism and creativity will help you evaluate which ideas will float to the top and which are runners-up. Being realistic keeps the seriously crazy ideas from being produced. It reminds us of the objectives of the project and forces us to accept its constraints. Being creative means pushing boundaries, taking risks, presenting ideas that are fresh and stand apart from the rest.

During your evaluation of the ideas from a brainstorm session, you must maintain balance. If you are too realistic you will be blind you to risky yet innovative solutions. However, being too creative could blind you to the communications challenges and objectives.

# Voice of Judgment

Now that you've evaluated the ideas developed during the brainstorm session, before moving forward with concept development, you have to determine which of the ideas should be further developed. At this point, you can provide the client with everything you know they are expecting to see. The alternative is to present them with ideas that you know will work, even if those ideas are not the ones the client wants. Your choices: be safe or be bold. Whether you know it or not, you are fighting what Mark Oldach calls the *Voice of Judgment* (VOJ).[5]

The VOJ is an inner voice driven by fear. It prevents you from pursuing innovative and unusual ideas with the confidence that you have something really good. This is the same voice that prevents us from presenting a risky concept to a client. When we do present risky ideas, we also present the "safe" idea because we are worried the client will accuse us of not listening. Sadly, many times the client will choose the safe idea, and you'll go back to the office angry because you didn't defend the more creative approach or because you never should have presented the safe idea in the first place.

If you know that the VOJ exists, you will be better prepared to deal with it. Oldach outlines the different forms the VOJ takes:

- The voice inside you that makes you afraid of pursuing creativity and that depresses you when you don't. This is the hardest one to overcome because we are our own worst critics. Ironically, reason and logic work best to overcome a personal fear. The often-asked question, "What is the worst that can happen if I present this idea?" usually produces an answer that is easy to deal with.

- The voices of others who have judged you unfairly; those voices in turn fuel the internal voice. These are the kind of people who get in the way of a good brainstorming session. Learning to ignore these voices is as important as squelching the internal voice.

- The voice of society that dictates etiquette, style, and in our case, "acceptable design approach." Creatives are exceptionally victim to this voice. We often wait until a design trend emerges before we consider it to be valid. We let others set the standards, and we track the standard by reading our design journals and annuals.

---

[5]Mark Oldarch. *Creativity for Graphic Designers* (Cincinnati: North Light Books, Inc., 1995), p. 82.

Creatives who succeed at by pursuing their ideas and dreams have the ability and confidence to control their own VOJ.

> *"A lifetime of mediocrity is a high price to pay for safety. Paranoia undoes greatness."*
>
> —Todd Henry, author

# Diamond in the Rough

Not all projects will provide you with obvious opportunities for creativity. It's easy to be creative for clients who appreciate your expertise and who provide you with exciting projects. The challenge for every great creative leader is to try and be creative for clients who have closed minds and are pains-in-the-ass to deal with. A truly great creative leader can treat all projects—all clients—as opportunities for creativity.

# In a Nutshell

As the creative lead, you should strive to create an environment that inspires creativity and values ideas. You can create an "idea culture" that values the process of perpetual idea generation and development, rather than one that's driven solely by the end product.[6] This type of environment breeds creative thinking and the continual improvement of an idea. Everyone contributes and feels like an important part of the process. No single individual has ownership of an idea because the idea was developed through the input of all members of the team. They will not fear providing input or worry about saying something stupid if collaboration is welcomed.

Now you've come to a fork in the road. Follow one direction, and you'll be taking the easy route. This route takes you to mediocrity. You will remain safely within the boundaries that have been set out for you. You don't push boundaries. No one will get frustrated with you. On most projects you've been there–done that, because you repeat everything and make every challenge fit within your little model of creativity. Your creative team will sail along with you until they find a place with a better creative leader who inspires and challenges them.

If you follow the second route, you will be challenged. You will strive to keep the generation of ideas fun and fresh and be a great creative lead. You will come up with concepts that make people think while also representing your

---

[6]Henry, Todd. *The Accidental Creative: How to Be Brilliant at a Moment's Notice* (New York: Penguin Group, 2011), p. 50.

client's brands appropriately. You will create an environment where your team feels safe to continually experiment and fail without fear. You will be sought out for your creativity and leadership skills. Songs will be sung of your exploits. Families will name their first-born children after you! A statue will be erected to commemorate your exploits… too much? Ok, just remove that last little bit, but you can be great.

Take your pick. Which way will you go? Go forth. Be fruitful and multiply… your ideas.

## BRAINSTORMING EXERCISES

The following are several exercises to help get your creative juices flowing.

### EXERCISE 1: RANDOM WORD

Making connections to random words can help open your mind to connections that you can make with your client's product, service, or organization. It opens your mind to new possibilities that might not be obvious if you were just trying to hammer out ideas on your own. It's important that the words be completely random and unrelated to your problem or challenge. This will force you to make a connection that isn't obvious.

There are several ways to ensure this. First, close your eyes and point your finger at the list of words provided on the next page. Write down the word you have selected. Second, close your eyes once more and point your finger at the list of words provided to select another word. Write it down. These are your random words.

Write down as many associations between these two words as you can. Break your words down into their characteristics. What is their function? What are their aesthetics? How are they used? What metaphors can be associated with them? What are the opposites of your words? Write down as many associated ideas and concepts as possible. If you get stuck, a thesaurus can help you find synonyms, antonyms, and other related words.

Now force connections between your random words and your problem or challenge, using the characteristics you identified in the previous step.

You can do this. Just remember:

- Don't reject a word just because you don't like it.

- Don't create too many steps between random words and the idea.

- Don't link the word to an idea you already have.

**Table 5-1.** Random Words

| Group 1 | Group 2 | Group 3 | Group 4 | Group 5 |
|---|---|---|---|---|
| Computer | Knife | Scissors | Air conditioner | Frog |
| Egg-beater | Forest | Tent | Cuckoo clock | Chocolate |
| Goldfish | Skyscraper | Prairie dog | Pillow | Garden |
| Rope | Hormones | Fruit cake | Cold cream | Garage |
| Beard | Comb | Sock | Hippopotamus | Husband |
| Toes | Toy | Soap | Curtains | Bowl |
| Telephone | Piano | Condom | Hamburger | Parking space |
| Floor | Map | Shark | Campfire | Jelly |
| Megaphone | Wire | Desert | Prawn | Ladder |
| Toothbrush | Diary | Pizza | VCR | Spotlight |
| Stamp | Snorkel | Earthquake | Eye drops | Chair |
| Bumblebee | Milk | Flag | Chess | Nose |
| Plan | CD | Coffin | Tennis racket | Elastic |
| Tissue paper | Transsexual | Drapes | Beer | Waterbed |
| Pencil | Mouse | Shop | Perfume | Drip tray |
| Book | Rattlesnake | In-tray | Baby food | Toaster |
| Band-Aid | Baby | Bicycle pump | Gel | Corkscrew |
| Teacher | Swamp | Pineapple | Soup | Hand towel |
| Rainforest | Nurse | Wheel | Umpire | Transformer |
| Apartment | Rose | Airport | Fins | Pickle |
| Alligator | Drawer | Teapot | Worm | TNT |
| Needle | Cave | Coffee grinder | Policeman | Fuel tank |
| Pasta | Motor oil | Chapstick | Magazine | Aqualung |
| Calendar | Wig | Sweet potato | Vitamin C | Woman |
| Orange | Football | Lozenge | Floppy disk | Cashew nut |
| Brick | Church | Wedding ring | Button | Balloon |
| Rock | Tiger | Gear stick | Paper cup | Tie rack |
| Greeting card | Scarf | Camel | DVD | Boxing ring |
| Television | Pimple | Seaweed | Ice cream | Glue |
| Jacket | Ticket | Handbag | Doorknob | Rug |

## EXERCISE 2: WHAT THE FLEEK?

"What the Fleek?" works by attaching your product or service to something that is already in the target audience's mind. Something that they feel is very hip and popular right now.

STEPS:

1. Who is your target? Describe them in at least three sentences. Provide details such as likes, dislikes, age, nationality, career field, and so on. Be as detailed as possible.

2. What interests your target? List at least 20 things.

3. Cross off everything related to your product or service.

4. Now, WHAT THE FLEEK? What grabs their attention or motivates your target? What is their current obsession?

5. Force a connection between your creative brief and the FLEEKING AWESOME item you've discovered. Answer this: How can I use the target market's interest/obsession with (WHAT THE FLEEK) to solve the challenge outlined in the creative brief?

## EXERCISE 3: EYES OF EXPERTS

This technique looks at the challenge presented to you from the point of view of another person—an expert from another field. You can use this to brainstorm alone or in groups.

Begin with selecting a number of prominent people from different fields. You can make your own list or you can use the list provided on the next page. Approach the problem imagining how you or your team believes each of the experts would handle it.

The key is to select people who

- Are experts of some sort.

- You know a lot about.

- You consider normal.

- Have a modus operandi or a particular way of working through their problems.

**Table 5-2.** Experts

| Hollywood | Superheroes | Sports | Historical | Characters |
|-----------|-------------|--------|------------|------------|
| Jennifer Lawrence | Batman | Ronda Rousey | Jesus | Homer Simpson |
| Robert Downey, Jr. | Superman | LeBron James | George Washington | Glenn Quagmire |
| Leonardo DiCaprio | Spiderman | Serena Williams | Anne Frank | Don Draper |
| Bradley Cooper | Nightwing | Cristiano Ronaldo | Martin Luther King, Jr. | Tony Soprano |
| Dwayne Johnson | Wonder Woman | Clayton Kershaw | Adolf Hitler | Fox Mulder |
| Hugh Jackman | Flash | J.J. Watt | Charles Darwin | Eric Cartman |
| Sandra Bullock | Robin | Stephen Curry | Julius Caesar | Joe Friday |
| Sofia Vergara | Supergirl | Aaron Rodgers | Michelangelo | Captain James T. Kirk |
| Scarlett Johansson | Black Canary | Pauline Ferrand-Prévot | Ronald Reagan | Spock |
| Chris Pratt | Black Panther | Miguel Cabrera | Sigmund Freud | Elaine Benes |
| Tom Hanks | Raven | Roger Federer | Joan of Arc | Stewie Griffin |
| Matt Damon | Batgirl | Tim Duncan | Queen Elizabeth | Frasier Crane |
| George Clooney | Hawkgirl | Eli Manning | Frida Kahlo | Kermit the Frog |
| Brad Pitt | Beast Boy | James Hardin | Florence Nightingale | Frank Underwood |
| Angelina Jolie | Cyborg | Manny Pacquiao | Mother Teresa | Jack Bauer |
| Kevin Hart | Starfire | Kevin Durant | Rosa Parks | Sherlock Holmes |
| Natalie Portman | The Hulk | Payton Manning | Sacagawea | Tyrion Lannister |

## EXERCISE 4: EXQUISITE CORPSE

This exercised is based on a collaborative word game called *Cadavre Exquis* (Exquisite Corpse). The game's roots can be linked to the Surrealist movement in Paris. There is some debate regarding whether it started in 1925 or 1928. Either way it works as a great way to get your minds thinking.

To play, the participants would start with a single piece of paper folded into halves or thirds. In turn, each participant would draw an image (or, on some occasions, paste an image down) on their section of the sheet of paper. When they finished they would fold the paper to conceal their contribution, and pass it on to the next player for his contribution.

Taking the basis of Exquisite Corpse and translating that into a brainstorming activity is easy. In this case, the idea is for a group of people to put together a sentence from words that may have little if any obvious relationship to each other.

For example, a sentence can be combined as follows:

- **FIRST** person chooses a definite or indefinite article and an adjective

- **SECOND** person chooses a noun

- **THIRD** person chooses a verb

- **FOURTH** person chooses another definite or indefinite article and an adjective

- **FIFTH** person chooses a noun

For example, "The gigantic buffalo sleeps steadfastly with stones."

The benefit of working with Exquisite Corpse is that the team has more words than those presented in Random Word to play with. The only limit is their ability to come up with words and their imaginations.

## EXERCISE 5: EXTREMES

This exercise is a useful technique to use when advertising a low-interest product or when the product benefits are minimal. It is also useful when promoting things that people take for granted.

Use this sentence to help ideate with this technique:

- (product) is so (benefit) that (exaggeration)

For example, "D'Antonio's new jeans are so sexy that Victoria's Secret sells them in the same section as lingerie."

or "George's Five Alarm Chili is so hot it's served by the fire department to ensure safety."

# Creative Exploration Tools

## Sketching and Thumbnails

Too many times, creatives begin their visual explorations on a computer before having ideas fully formed. They worry about fonts, colors, and images before they even have a concept. Why do so many creatives skip a critical step in the ideation process and begin working on the computer so quickly? This, in my opinion, is due to either a lack of creative confidence or bad habits that were developed during their time in school or as young professionals. They start working with the end in mind rather than thinking beyond the obvious. They sometimes gravitate to familiar solutions that have worked for them in the past. Without careful consideration, this method of idea development may result in ideas that could be off-brand or off-target.

Why do I believe this? First, because I strongly believe that ideas developed in haste on the computer have a tendency to look too polished very early in the game. Second, because the hastily created concepts will most likely be piggybacking ideas that a designer was intentionally or unintentionally

© Eleazar Hernández 2017

E. Hernández, *Leading Creative Teams*, DOI 10.1007/978-1-4842-2056-6_6

influenced by as they surfed the Web to visit creative websites (creativity-online.com, adsoftheworld.com, luerzersarchive.com, etc.) or flipped through *Communication Arts*, *HOW*, or *PRINT* annuals. Third, creatives sometimes feel the pressure of having to maintain a certain level of billability so they strive to knock out as much as they can in as little time as possible without taking the steps necessary to produce truly incredible work.

If your team is working up ideas by jumping directly onto the computer, sadly, in most cases they will spend hours trying to "polish a turd" in the hopes that the client will like something they have worked up. As creative lead, you should retrain your creatives to go about this process much differently. Get them to slow down at the beginning of the ideation process because in the end, the only idea that will see the light of day is the one that solves a client's marketing challenge.

Let's examine one of the greatest techniques you can encourage your team to utilize as they work up their ideas—thumbnail sketching.

# What Are Thumbnail Sketches?

Thumbnails are small-scale drawings whose primary function is to gather a lot of ideas on paper in a very short amount of time. In other words, thumbnail sketches are miniature drawings. I believe it's one of the best ways to visually brainstorm because you should be focusing on overall concepts and layout massing instead of obsessing over elements such as fonts, colors, and specific imagery, the things that really don't matter at the inception of a project.

When your team is thumbnailing they should simply let the ideas flow. This is not practice for honing their drawing skills; instead their focus should be on idea generation. Thumbnail sketches are quick and even somewhat sloppy, using basic shapes to make ideas visible (Figure 6-1). Your creative team should not spend too long on a single image. As soon as they get a feel for what the basic layout idea might look like, they should move along to the next idea.

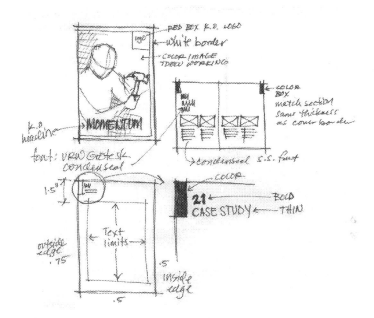

**Figure 6-1.** Annual report thumbnail sketch

# Why Is Thumbnailing a Good Thing?

To understand the benefits that come from pages of small, quickly drawn sketches, just consider the tunnel vision that results from skipping this step. When creatives rush to the computer to begin creating, they frequently produce the first thing that pops into their heads. In their rush to complete the task, they will work the assignment until it is nearly complete. This course of action results in knee-jerk ideas that result in creative solutions that are generally not very original or insightful and that lack the spark of insight that shows a true understanding of the client's unique marketing position. The problem with this is that you can pretty much bet that the first idea your creative team produces is also the same first idea anyone would have when they are not taking the time to brainstorm ideas and develop unique solutions.

What's worse, they tend to fall in love with the idea and will defend it as if it were a good solution. Don't worry: it's natural for them to feel this way. Our ideas are our babies. When we spend time nurturing one, it's very difficult to just leave it behind—even when it doesn't fully meet with the client's expectation.

The main flaw with initial computer ideation is that the lack of critical thought put into idea generation. By "critical thought" I mean real in-depth criticism and logical reasoning. Instead, your creatives will come up with three quick ideas that seem viable, convince themselves that they've done their due diligence, and then decide which one of those three they can convince you to sell to your client. They might have been able to come up with ten ideas that were better suited for your client, but because they didn't take the time to thumbnail at the beginning and work through several different directions, they just presented whatever they could throw your way.

Thumbnail sketching forces creatives to exercise our brainpower to tap into real creative thought by producing as many different variations of a concept as possible. With this method you have the benefit of looking at everything you can possibly think of and then making an intelligent decision about which ideas are worth pursuing and which ideas need to be dropped. If members of your team come up with similar thumbnail sketches, it could indicate that the idea is an obvious one that anyone could come up with. Eliminate it and encourage them to expand their thinking to less common ideas.

# The Role of Sketching During the Ideation Phase

As a tool or skill, sketching has its role in the design process. That role varies depending on the end product being created, the size and scope of the project, the individual designer's style, experience, and workflow, and the client's expectations.

A large project with a significant client budget will benefit from sketching throughout the ideation process. This ensures that before a massive amount of time is invested in refining a solution, a direction is first agreed upon with the client. Sketching can begin as loose gestural scribbles that display basic concepts then work their way into more detailed visual compositions. The sketching can eventually lead to more refined thumbnails after the initial direction is chosen.

For smaller projects, you may work up your sketches during your initial ideation phase, but because of the smaller budget you may not sketch as extensively. You can work through your sketches quickly and then begin to build your comprehensive designs on the computer. With quick designs you can begin to experiment with type styles and comp photos.

## Save Time

I know. I know. You think you don't have time to thumbnail. You need to get the job done quickly because you have a bunch of deadlines and other client work to get started on or complete. Your team might say they can't draw or they aren't comfortable using pencil and paper to come up with ideas. Maybe they'll lament that they weren't taught how to thumbnail in school. I call bullshit on most of those excuses. If done correctly thumbnail sketching can actually improve your timeline rather than blow it.

First of all, you don't have to spend an entire day thumbnailing. All you need to do is dedicate a specific amount of time to idea generation. It could be ten minutes, an hour, three hours—whatever amount of time you want to spend. It's up to you. Second, brainstorming can help end procrastination on a project. Procrastination often occurs because you are unsure of the assignment or your ability to find a solution. If you engage your brain and begin thinking through ideas by thumbnailing, you'll find that once you've landed an idea, you can knock out a design much quicker and more confidently than if you had simply jumped onto your computer first.

When creatives begin brainstorming on the computer they typically spend time searching through thousands of fonts. They will work through a color palette that reinforces the job's visuals. They spend hours searching through stock photo sites to find an image that will help lead them to a solution. These are all tasks that—although important for the completion of the assignment—should not be considered until a strong concept or direction is determined.

# Developing Skills That Communicate Ideas Effectively

One of the saddest things I have encountered with the latest generation of creatives joining the fray is their lack of ability and desire to sketch. They not only don't want to sketch, but they shudder at the idea of being asked to scribble up ideas. They lack motivation, and often times, don't understand its value. That's sad, man. Just sad.

Take heart, true believer, you don't have to have the sketching ability of Michelangelo. As a matter of fact, if you can't draw, you may have an easier time than people who fancy themselves "auh-teests." Repeat after me: "*It's not about beauty, it's about the idea. It's not about the beauty, it's about the idea.*" I have witnessed creatives who consider themselves accomplished artists spending more time generating fewer thumbnails simply because they want to make sure every line is straight, every circle is perfect, every typeface is correctly represented, and so on. They strive for perfection because they feel they will be judged by their thumbnails; however, that's not the purpose of thumbnail sketches. They are simply a quick way to generate lots of ideas in a short amount of time. The scribble shown in Figure 6-2 was created while my copywriting partner and I discussed ideas for an upcoming client proposal.

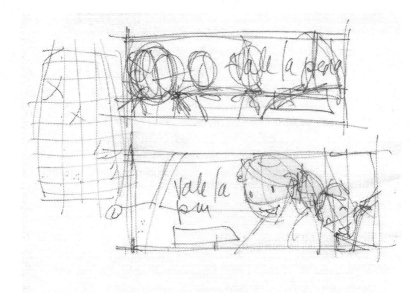

**Figure 6-2.** Don't spend time trying to make thumbnails perfect. They simply need to be able to communicate an idea

The key is quantity over quality. I have nothing against great-looking thumbnails. In fact, I love checking out thumbnails and comparing them to the final product, but great artistic skills are not necessary to generate great ideas. Whether your creative team members are accomplished artists or a novice scribblers, make sure they remember that their goal is to get all of their ideas out and onto the paper.

## No Tweaking

Don't spend lots of time tweaking an idea to get it just right. If it's not coming out the way you want it, bag it. If you start sketching an idea and realize that you hate it, resist the urge to erase it and start over. As a matter of fact, don't use pencils to thumbnail; use a pen. That way you've not tempted to mess around with perfecting ideas at this stage. Maybe in a few hours you'll look back on that sketch and see a solid idea in there. If not, be glad you moved on.

## Happiness in Multiples

How many is too many? When you're generating thumbnails, don't stop at five or six. As a creative lead, you better have a lot more ideas rolling around in your cabeza than that. My undergraduate design professor, Louis Ocepek, had us generate 100 or more unique thumbnails for every single project. This is a number I have asked for from several teams in the past. Why? Because it works.

At least once, I'd like you to try and scribble out 100 thumbnails. Spend the time and try to get as close to 100 as possible. By the time you get to 25, you will believe there is nothing left in your head (Figure 6-3). If you push through to 40, you will be mentally exhausted. If you get beyond 40 you will be running on fumes, but the ideas will be coming from deep inside your cabeza. You might produce ideas that you had never even imagined because you're too tired to censor yourself or worry about what others have done in the past. Try it at least once and see what you come up with.

**Figure 6-3.** Multiple typographic logo thumbnails

## Repetition Is Not a Good Thing

When faced with the challenge of producing many thumbnails, you might start by working through tiny variations of the same idea. While this practice is typically what we have to do to develop logo ideas, when developing ideas for other advertising or collateral materials it is a somewhat worthless practice.

You should be focusing on trying to come up with truly unique concepts. You can do it. Push your brain to produce concepts that are as different from each other as you can manage. Remember, this is brainstorming so there is no such thing as a bad idea. Have fun with it. Be weird. Go crazy.

# Archive Your Thumbnails

If at all possible, save your thumbnails. As you proceed into the project, you might want or need to look back on them to ensure that you are staying true to your original concept. As projects progress, you might lose your focus and need to be reminded of where your idea started. Worst-case scenario, your client might dislike the direction you've taken and you may need to go back to the drawing board. It's a good thing you have many thumbnail sketches to refer back to. They could provide a great springboard for more ideas.

Beyond keeping your thumbnails for a project, consider archiving them in more permanent forms. I have all of the hardbound sketchbooks I used for thumbnails, notes, and sketches in my office. For the thumbnails I have created on marker paper, I have an archival, acid-free museum box that I purchased many years ago to house those scribbles. Sometimes it's nice to go back and visit my little nuggets of inspiration to see how things may have changed in my own creative development process.

# Five Uses for Thumbnail Sketching

Typically, most creatives think of thumbnail sketches for use in generating layout ideas, but the practice is beneficial in most types of design. Sitting down with a pencil and sketching out dozens of ideas may seem like a very natural first step in logo generation, so why not apply this same technique to just about everything you design?

Logo design, headline type treatments, web pages, brochures, business cards, app interfaces, and character design are just a few of the tasks that can benefit from thumbnail sketching (Figure 6-4).

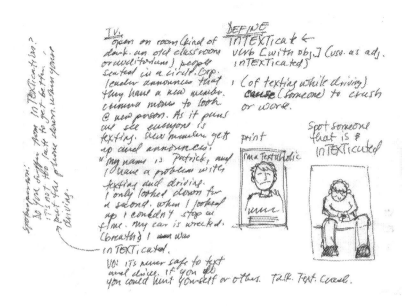

**Figure 6-4.** Thumbnails can start as a quick idea and a written thought

While there are many categories in which thumbnails can be utilized, the following is a review of five of them that immediately come to mind.

# 1. Concept Development

Sketching is an excellent way to quickly explore concepts. A couple of hours spent on concept development can help lead toward solutions for the marketing or design challenge you're trying to address. Concept development is one of the most important steps in the design process. As previously mentioned, working through concepts on paper at the beginning of a project can help save time when compared to spending time trying to develop concepts on the computer.

To demonstrate an example of thumbnail sketching for concept development:

After being commissioned to develop a logo for Houses in San Antonio, a local real estate company, I explored more than 60 initial thumbnails sketches before narrowing the concepts down to just a handful of what I believed were the best visual solutions (Figure 6-5). During this phase, I explored iconic imagery, typography, and layout.

**Figure 6-5.** Sampling of the marks developed during the ideation of Houses in San Antonio's logo

I then worked through several ideas. Through the use of thumbnails, I was able to work quickly and generate a multitude of ideas in a relatively short period of time. Because I initiated this assignment with thumbnail sketches I was able to generate and evaluate many ideas to determine which—if any—merited further exploration. Once I selected a few thumbnails that I believed were strong solutions that could be presented to the client, I moved to the computer to develop the marks (Figure 6-6).

**Figure 6-6.** Initial marks developed from thumbnail sketches

While computer programs are great for executing work, in my opinion, thinking on paper with a pencil or marker is always the place to start. Don't rely on a software program to be the basis of your creative output. Practice good design… have a concept.

**Remember: A computer program does not make a designer.**

## 2. Composition or Layout

Thumbnail sketches are a quick way to create a basic composition for web sites, ads, out-of-home, brochures, posters, and so on to quickly evaluate layout choices. You can make a series of thumbnail sketches in various sizes to suit your purposes. As long as your sketches capture the necessary elements, you're good to go.

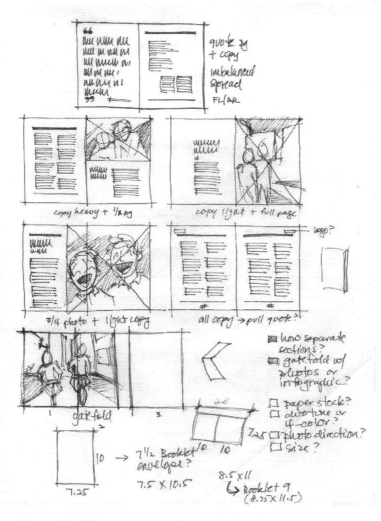

**Figure 6-7.** Massing studies for a multipage brochure project

Thumbnail sketches can be used for massing studies or general blocking sketches that show overall positioning of objects (Figure 6-7). I create massing studies when I am working up the layouts for web pages. This helps me determine the overall visual hierarchy of the page and how I would like to guide a viewer through the information. I utilize thumbnails for my massing studies before I work through the actual elements on the web page.

# 3. Communication and Approval

While some agency people shy away from this, showing sketched thumbnails or compositions to clients can potentially save you a lot of time during the creative process. Some will say "the client won't be able to visualize what you're showing." I do not agree with that mindset. As a creative lead, do not fall into the trap of thinking that your clients can't visualize the beginning of an idea from a sketch. Keep in mind that in the case of showing your sketches to a client, it is not mandatory that you have more "polished" drawing ability to display your idea, but it doesn't hurt if you do. This is in fact a case when you will need to have drawing ability to show your conceptual scribbles to the client for them to really grasp what you've created.

Showing your clients sketches can save you time. For example, if you, a creative team member, or one of your freelancers is going to spend hours on an illustration for a client project you want to make sure that the client is in agreement with the direction before moving forward. Getting approvals from clients is an important part of the creative process. I believe it can be done with thumbnail sketches—good ones. The more detailed the project the more I recommend securing client approval early.

Here's how it would work in a perfect world: The art director and copywriter have brainstormed several idea for a project. The art director works out concepts and presents to the creative director (CD). The CD takes the sketches and presents them to the account team. If they are in accord with the scribbles, they go on to present the concepts to the client for approval of the creative direction. The client approves artwork before it goes to the next stage of development. This process saves time by solidifying an idea before going on to more advanced stages in the development of elements.

# 4. Visual Exploration

Sketching out ideas can be used as a journaling activity to record and explore your thoughts, interests, and plans. There are many types and sizes of sketchbooks available to you. Throughout my career I have made a habit of utilizing hardbound sketchbooks. Hardbound sketchbooks give you a safe place to place your notes and sketches that will last for years. Because of the hardbound cover, the pages are bound inside and they won't fall out they way they do in some of the less expensive perfect-bound versions. You also don't have to worry about a spiral getting flattened, which is a problem with spiral-bound sketchbooks. I have used sketchbooks that range from the cheap black books with white pages to Moleskines. They have ranged in size from small, pocket-sized books to 11×17-inch monsters. No matter the size, the key is to have a sketchbook with at all times. You never know when you will be inspired.

I have heard from novice sketchbookers that they worry about ruining their sketchbook with their bad sketches or random notes. They stress about marking on the pristine pages. I feel your pain. There is nothing like the beauty of a bright white page in a perfectly bound sketchbook. Oh, the smell of a new book or the feel of the toothy page. Ah, the heaven. The sweet, nerdy, creative heaven. Oh so good. While I understand your feelings about making that first mark in your book or continuing to use the book for any and every scribble, I don't censor what I place in my books. They are repositories for ideas. My sketchbooks have always been the storehouse for my ideas. Whether I'm laying out a brochure, working up the user interface for a webpage, or quickly running through explorations for a logo design, my books are filled with ideas—good and bad.

A benefit of using hardbound sketchbooks is you can refer back to them. You can see your own creative process and remember things about your life during the period when you were knocking out those ideas. I have sketchbooks that date back to the late 1980s. No, we weren't writing on animal hide back then. We actually used paper. As I flip through those books, I can remember the thoughts that went into those scribbles. You never know, you might be inspired in the future by a scribble or mark that you make today.

Here is a quick list of some of the items found in my sketchbooks:

- *Ideas that I had to get out of my head quickly.* Sometimes I just need to get everything out just to clear my head and prepare for the next task.

- *Scribbles to explain an idea.* When I am brainstorming with a team, I am drawing as we work through different ideas. To be able to explain what I'm thinking, I find that I can do a better job if I scribble the ideas to give them a visual reference for what I'm trying to explain.

- *Directions for art directors or production artists.* When I don't have time to create initial InDesign or Illustrator files, I rely on other creatives to execute from a sketch. I create quick scribbles that have enough information to get them started and depend on them to see it through to fruition.

- *Visuals to quickly get the creative team on the same page.* When I am working with a larger group, if initial brand standards or a style guide have not been created for a client, I like to work through the visuals on a whiteboard with everyone involved in attendance. This is one way to get everyone on board while explaining the visual vocabulary for a client's project.

- *Initial concepts prior to starting an illustration.* If I have received an illustration commission or I am working it into a design gig, I will work up the initial concepts as sketches to get sign-off by the client before going to the computer.

- *Sketches to provide general conceptual explorations to a client.* I sometimes like to give a client a preview of the creative work via a sketch. This is one way to give them a hint of the direction a project is going without showing them too much. This is something I do only with clients who get hung up on minutia very early in the creative process. Sometimes you can ease them into a creative solution by means of a sketch.

## 5. Refining Visual Solutions

The design process involves a series of visual refinements. Once a direction has been determined for an assignment, you can continue to refine the visuals through tighter sketches. Once you're confident that you've taken it as far as you can, it's time to head to the computer or hand it off to one of your art directors or production team to take care of developing the work digitally. Now the process of sketching moves into digital drafts.

# Things to Consider When Thumbnailing

When (not if) you're knocking out pencil sketches or if you are already utilizing them, here are eight simple things to consider:

- Use a grid.

- Keep your thumbnails in proportion to the actual size of the job.

- Utilize shorthand for type (serif vs. sans-serif, leading, justification etc.).

- Don't worry about images with loose sketches.

- Provide a contact sheet for images with tighter versions of the layouts.

- Try different concepts to reach the client's objectives and target market, not just variations of the same idea.

- Be original, be creative, and have fun.

# Visual Shorthand for Creative Communication: Examples

Although you don't want to stress about how your thumbnails are arranged on your page, you might want to consider keeping them arranged in a grid. What I have found works best for me is utilizing 9×12-inch Bienfang Graphics 360 100% rag translucent marker paper. I have been utilizing Bienfang pads almost as long as I have used hardbound sketchbooks.

The beauty of using the Beinfang pad for thumbnails is you can place a piece of 1/4" graph paper underneath the page and use it to help you keep your sketches proportional. This is beneficial for you to design in proportion to the final layout. Figure 6-8 shows some of the shorthand marks I use when creating my thumbnails.

A visual shorthand system can help you get your ideas out quickly and concisely. When you develop a system that works for you, you will be able to quickly jot down your ideas without having to worry about how you'll remember to decipher your notes in the future. In addition, when you work with your team and they understand your visual shorthand you can leave notes or provide direction to them without having to explain every mark on the page. They will understand the difference between the shorthand for a headline versus body copy. They will be able to tell the proportions of the ad that you'd like them to create. Don't worry about following the examples I have provided in the following. You create a system that works for you. Be consistent with it and be sure to teach your team what the symbols are so they will understand what you're trying to communicate to them.

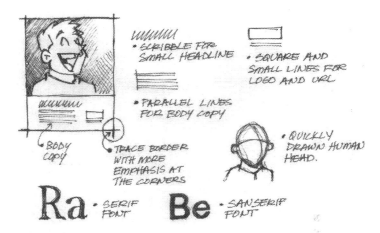

**Figure 6-8.** Thumbnail shorthand

# In a Nutshell

You may feel the overwhelming desire to skip working through your ideation process with thumbnail sketching and jump straight to the computer. Resist the urge. There is no quicker method for exploring multiple visual solutions than sketching. The larger an assignment, the more concepts you and your team will need to develop, the more thumbnail sketching will help you.

Putting your initial ideas into thumbnail sketches might feel like a pain at first, but once you get into the habit you'll find that it's not only enjoyable, but in terms of your creativity it's also a worthwhile exercise.

While I am obviously a huge proponent of thumbnail sketching, I recognize that no matter what I say there will be creatives who simply do not feel there is any value in it. I ask that you at least consider it and try it for several weeks. You may be surprised to find that you like it. If, however, you have tried it for several weeks, and it's just not something you or your team find is a valuable way to brainstorm and develop ideas, bag it. Don't stress over it. Maybe you're one of those rare people who can jump on the computer and make magic.

▓ **Just For Fun**   Challenge yourself or a workmate to a race. One of you can use the computer while the other simply uses a pencil and paper. Your challenge is to develop four quick layouts of a poster for an event. Here is your creative brief:

Assignment: The Lake Titicaca Cultural Center is sponsoring a concert on the 5$^{th}$ of July. The band "Renegade Nuns on Wheels" is playing. The warm-up band is "the BLT Sammys." Renegade Nuns on Wheels is known for their energetic acid rock style as well as their attire: camouflage nuns' habits. They love black and white (of course), but also like to add red for a little shock.

Parameters: 11×17-inch poster, 1-color with bleeds

This is it! The big shebang! In the red corner we have a designer with a computer. In the blue corner, we have a designer with a Sharpie and a marker pad. Each of you now has the same information. Give yourselves 10 minutes and see who can complete the assignment first or who can come up with more design ideas. Ready? Go!

# The Art of the Critique

## How to evaluate your team's work constructively

Any creative who tells you that they don't have a personal attachment to the work they produce is lying to you. When we create solutions to marketing challenges, we do so from a very personal basis. Sure, we use research or client information provided to us to come up with creative solutions, but regardless of where the information came from, the act of creating is always personal. We pour a little bit of ourselves into every project. The reality is that all designers, art directors, copywriters, illustrators, and so on infuse a little bit of their personality and aesthetics in all their work.

Because your team will consider their ideas and creations their babies—those cute little nuggets of creative thought that were once glimmers in their eyes who have grown, developed, and been placed on display full-frontal to the world—we must be cognizant of how we provide feedback about them. This chapter will go over ways to effectively evaluate—or critique (crit)—your team's work. Critiquing work is important skill creative directors must develop because it can help the creative process. Likewise, neglecting to critique work or critiquing in a negative way can hinder the creative process.

© Eleazar Hernández 2017

E. Hernández, *Leading Creative Teams*, DOI 10.1007/978-1-4842-2056-6_7

Creatives who have survived design school or a creative sequence can sympathize with the pain that a critique can cause. When work is being critiqued, your team may feel as if their work is coming under attack. This is not the way to critique work. Critiques should be viewed as a positive aspect of the creative process. Your team should be inspired to go back and make edits. They should be challenged to try and adjust some of the content based on insights given during a critique. This chapter will help you ensure your critiques are neither horrific nor pointless (filled with unwarranted praise). Before we go into the process of critiquing, let's go over a basic question: Why critique in the first place?

# Why Critique?

The answer should be fairly obvious. As a creative lead, you cannot expect your team to adequately solve marketing challenges without the benefit of your insight or critique. There are independent or work-for-hire designers in the world (I refuse to use the f-word) or people who get into the creative field without formal training who knock things out on their own. They concept alone. They design alone. They judge their work and make edits alone. The problem with this singular frame of reference is that their ideas are limited to their specific knowledge and experience. I have always said, "Two heads are better than one. Four heads are better than two." This thinking holds true for brainstorming, determining a design direction, and of course, critiquing work. It's difficult to know if your work is the best it can be if you work alone and have no one to look at your work and provide constructive feedback.

Please understand that critiquing work isn't a chance to tell someone how you would've designed the piece had you created it. It's also not an opportunity to tell them that "not only does their design lack inspiration, but their mama dresses them funny." The goal of a critique is to provide constructive feedback that inspires your creatives to polish up the work and explore alternate ways to solve the problem. A properly executed critique will allow your creative team to gain insights and perspectives beyond what they are capable of coming up with on their own. As a result it will push them to produce better solutions for your clients.

## Are internal critiques with your account service team necessary?

Whether you are a creative lead in an agency or design studio, you are responsible for ensuring that the work produced by your team not only addresses a client's needs, but also measures up to the standards of your organization.

Some creative leads really could care less what their teammates in Account Service have to say. They believe that the account executives (AEs) are mindless drones who merely pass on information from the client to the creative team. This couldn't be further from the truth. Your AEs are the first line of communication. They are well-versed in what the client objectives are. You should take every opportunity to solicit information and opinions from your AEs. Ultimately the responsibility for deciding what to show the client rests on your shoulders, but do not make the mistake of thinking of yourself as a solitary creative island. Trust your AEs to help you navigate the sometimes choppy client waters to give your creative work an even better chance of surviving.

## Is there value to internal critiques before showing work to the client?

An internal review of the creative work before it goes to the client is the best way to ensure your team is producing work that will address client challenges. Critiques are an excellent tool that should be included as a routine step in your creative development process.

Internal reviews conducted prior to presenting work to a client have quantitative and qualitative benefits which include the following:

- Improves creativity
- Elevates the quality of the work
- Safeguards against "cookie-cutter" or completely wacked solutions that are strategically unsound
- Ensures the messaging targets the right audience
- Detects deficiencies early, allowing time for correction and improvement

# How to Receive a Critique: A Grain of Salt

Everyone has to answer to someone. Even you, my friend. As creative lead you will receive critiques from agency management teammates as well as current and potential clients. When you are on the receiving end of a critique, it's important to take both the bad and good feedback in stride. Remember that creativity isn't math. There are no absolutely formulas to determine whether a creative idea is good or bad; there are only subjective opinions that may differ from one person to another. You need to be as receptive to criticism as you expect your team to be. Model the correct behavior.

That said, remember to focus on the reason for the critique—making your team's work the best it can be. If you disagree with specific feedback, explain what the rationale was that led to the work in a thoughtful manner. You must also listen to what is being said. Try not to get defensive or take someone's criticisms personally.

## Why Do Creatives Avoid Critiques?

Creative teams generally cringe at the idea of critiques. More often than not, critiques are unorganized, unfocused, waste time, and don't provide any real value. Some creatives fear evaluation because they don't feel comfortable explaining their rationale or worse yet, they actually don't have a rationale for their work. Others have experienced extremely harsh critiques that were not helpful or productive. Those who avoid critiques do so because they see them as an attempt at "policing" their work, which makes them feel as if they have no control.

As the creative director, remember that the members of your team insert their hearts and souls into developing their concepts, and they will generally take criticism personally if not done in a constructive way. When offering input, put yourself in their shoes, making sure your feedback is direct, simple, and tactful. Be specific on what works and what doesn't work. If you don't do this, you will demoralize your team and they will be less likely to be motivated to do their best work (Figure 7-1).

**Figure 7-1.** Critiquing your team's work is a skill that must be developed

To help your team suppress their flight-or-fight response when faced with a critique, here is what *you* want to avoid:

- **Too much direction**—nobody likes to have a dictator telling them what to do.

- **Intimidation**—don't be a jerk about it.

- **Being tactless**—you will appear as if your judgment is subjective instead of objective.

- **Biased direction**—will cause dissension among the ranks causing strife among your creative team.

- **Pushing your own creative agenda**—squashes any motivation your team has to do their own work

## Who Else Can Critique Work?

Try asking someone who is unfamiliar with the project to critique. They can come to the table having the benefit of not knowing what the task was or what the impetus was behind your solution. Sometimes an uninvolved third party can come up with insights and suggestions you haven't considered before.

## Who Is Really in the Hot Seat?

As the creative director, you may be feeling lots of pressure to come up with great suggestions, but keep in mind the person being critiqued is in a much more difficult position than the person doing the critiquing. A key insight to keep in mind is that every design has at least one good feature. You'll have plenty of time to get to the things you think should be changed. Just make sure that you don't make it up — be honest about what you do like, because no one wants to be patronized. In the following, I discuss that ways to critique positively.

# Where Do You Begin?

It can sometimes seem daunting when you have a pile of work in front of you or hung on a wall to review. You may feel a bit overwhelmed. Breathe. Start by looking and listening. Look at the work. Ask questions. What information is being presented to you by your creative team? Are you looking at the work alone? Do you have the creative brief in front of you? Is your team providing you with a brief overview of their rationale for the work? What was their intention and inspiration?

Look at the work. Take it in. Analyze it. Ask questions.

# The Truth Hurts... Sometimes

A good critique typically involves both positive and negative feedback, which can be tricky to navigate. Just as it's important to strike the right balance of feedback, it's important to give it in the right way. The sections that follow go over some common errors to spare you and your creatives the pain of enduring poorly delivered critiques.

## "I Would Have Designed It Like This" Critique

Whether a design studio or advertising agency, the environment can occasionally be a somewhat hostile one. Creatives tend to be a competitive bunch who are in a constant state of competition. They are looking at their own work and comparing it to other work being produced by teammates. They are competing for recognition, awards, promotions, and overall growth in the department. Toss in a little designer moodiness and you've got a great recipe for hurt feelings, misunderstandings, and resistance to suggestions. Remember, even when we all receive the same information in the creative brief, because we are individuals, we will come up with different solutions. Yes, one team member would solve a marketing challenge differently than another, but that doesn't mean each idea doesn't have its own merits or that the ideas should be completely dismissed just because they weren't executed the way you would have done. Don't allow this "my way is the right way" rationale to serve as the fuel for this type of critique.

## "Dive-Bomber" Critique

Many creative spaces are set in open environments. Open environments encourage collaboration and interaction. Another positive aspect of open environments is they keep people from spending their days on Facebook, Twitter, and Instagram. Sounds like a great idea, right? Uh, sure. But there are also drawbacks.

It's pretty common for any member of the agency to pass your work station, see a design, and provide unsolicited critiques such as, "Wow, I don't like that," or "I have an idea of how you can make that better." These random comments can be really annoying to your team as they work. Ask your agency mates to resist the urge to dive-bomb and kill your team's ideas as they pass by. Your team is working through their process, and receiving unsolicited critiques while they design is neither constructive nor informative.

## "Vague and Pointless" Critique

If the main point of a critique is to provide clear, constructive criticism that gives your creative team the ammunition to go back and improve their concept, then the vague and pointless (VP) critique is the exact opposite. The VP critique can range from overly dramatic ("OMG! I hate Zapfino! So many people are using that font on everything!"), to the simply unimportant ("I really think this looks kind of plain. Could you make it more designy?"). Remind your team (or agency mates who might take part in a crit) if they absolutely hate what they are seeing, it's best to temper their comments. They can find a way to provide feedback on a less-than-favorable piece of work without completely demoralizing your creative team.

# Critique the Right Way

Too many times, critiques fall into the what-not-to-do categories listed above. Why? Because people were never taught how to provide meaningful and useful feedback that inspires action. The basic technique is pretty simple: You start out saying something you like about the design to help put the designer at ease. Then move onto what you think could be improved. Phrase this in a constructive way — if something isn't coming across as intended, let the designer know how it could be done better. The sections that follow offer a couple more hints that should help you critique in a positive way.

## Understand the Parameters of the Assignment

If you are critiquing work and you don't know what the client's needs, objectives, and goals are, have your team give you a brief introduction to put them in context. Without some kind of insight into the marketing or communications challenges that are being addressed, your insight will be baseless and somewhat unhelpful. For example, you recommend that your team remove the color red from a design because it feels angry, only to find out red is the client's brand color. In these cases, it's better if you keep your comments and opinions to yourself than to recommend something that isn't within the scope of the project.

## Start with a Positive

To get things off on the right foot, I recommend starting your critique with at least three things you like about the work being presented. Providing positive feedback can help bolster the confidence of your creatives and help them to be more receptive to any changes or criticisms you might have. Starting with at least three positive things also makes you dig deeper into your mind and move away from providing gut reactions. Don't ever base a critique on your personal preferences. Honestly, nobody cares what you like or don't like. You will most likely not be in the target demographic so you need to keep your opinions objective and based on rational thought. Critiques based on research and insights will separate opinions from fact and open a dialog.

## What Would You Improve?

You can't simply run into a critique and toss grenades at everyone's work. In other words, you can't just list everything you don't like about someone's design. You should limit your discussion to what you think can be improved upon in the work. This helps keep the conversation fluid and it opens up a dialogue on the design. Additionally, it allows you to relay information to your team in a way that will give them the tools and means to improve their concept. Point out things like cliché phrases, and give tips on color palettes and their effect on mood, visual balance, white space, hierarchy, and so on.

## If You Love It, Let Them Know

One of the worst things you can do is constantly provide negative feedback. When you do this your team will come to loathe your critiques. Don't keep your focus on the negative aspects of what you're reviewing. If you like something say so. Tell your creative team what you like and why you like it, and then wait for their response. This doesn't mean you should praise poor work because it's easier than offering insight or because you're afraid of offending someone. Unnecessary praise can be as harmful as harsh criticism.

Keep the techniques outlined in this chapter in mind for more successful critiques with your creative team. If you do, they will appreciate your honesty without resenting the feedback you provide.

## Know When to Draw the Line

Something that drives me crazy is when a critic begins their commentary with, "I like…" Any statement beginning with "I" is already too narrow. The person who should be helping you is now internalizing and making their opinions, likes, and dislikes part of their insight and feedback. There is a difference between a personal opinion and an unbiased critique. Make sure you separate the two.

Here's a hint: start your sentence with the phrase, "I believe this does/doesn't work as a solution to the assignment because…" This simple way of framing your critique, moves any statement you make away from a personal "I like or dislike" message to one that judges the work based on whether or not it solves the problem posed in the creative brief.

# Give Them Something to Do

Give actionable critiques! If you know an alternative way to accomplish something, let your creatives know. Don't just tell them what is wrong and expect them to go fix it. Give them ideas or point them in a direction that will help them develop solutions. Even if your team does not go with your suggestion verbatim, it could help them come up with their own solution to the problem.

# Keep Things Objective: Stick to the Creative Brief

Use the creative brief to establish a context for critiques. The creative brief positions the work in the context of the assignment's objectives and gives you a tool for judging the effectiveness of the creative solutions. If you don't use a creative brief as your measuring stick, the work will be judged on personal preference and ultimately result in meaningless feedback. Utilizing the creative brief as a measuring tool allows you to

- Reiterate the problem to ensure the assignment objectives are not lost between the kick-off meeting and the critique.

- Connect the challenge to objectives and address how the solution ties back to objectives.

- Demonstrate how the problem was solved and support your creative recommendations with data points.

# Critiques Should Evolve

Typically when a project is in its beginning stages, the critique goals and questions will be much different than when critiquing a project that is in its later phases. In the beginning there shouldn't be micro-focus on the details. The questions and goals should help paint a picture with broad strokes.

Questions could include the following:

- What are the main concerns that the client wants to address?

- Are those concerns being adequately considered with these solutions?

Typical goals for these early critiques might include the following:

- Obtain specific kinds of feedback about a set of different design approaches

- Compare how several elements could work together

- Discuss how the target audience will work through a design
- Explore marketing solutions of competitors
- Ask teammates with different job functions to provide feedback based on their expertise

As the project timeline progresses, the tone of the critique should change. There should be more solidified concepts and visuals to review.

During the later stages, the scope of the critique discussion should be decreased because issues and questions have already been resolved. Critiques at the later stages of a project should move to focusing on grammar, spelling, punctuation, color modes (CMYK vs. RGB), clarity of concept and imagery, use of specific typefaces, and so on.

# Materials and Rooms

Depending on the kinds of designs you'll be critiquing and the goals you have, you will want to handle any materials and the room you are critiquing in differently. The way you have the work displayed could significantly impact how it is received. In other words, you should not present work that will be presented to the general public in print via digital means and, in contrast, you should not present web banners as printouts. The following are several quick guidelines for the way in which you should consider presenting work to be critiqued.

## Printed Work

For critiques of printed work (brochures, posters, direct mail, ads, etc.), printed samples of all elements to hand out to each person will work fine. There is some debate regarding whether elements should be rendered in a somewhat finished state or if they can be sketched. The manner in which you have the work presented should be based on the visualization skills of the people critiquing. If there are other creatives in the room who can visualize finished projects by merely looking at scribbles and talking through ideas, then sketches will work fine. If you are in a room full of people who do not have the visualization ability to see beyond the scribble to imagine the finished product, then you should present work that is mocked-up to appear almost final.

## Out-of-Home

A print of all out-of-home (OOH) executions, such as billboards, bus wraps transit shelter posters and so on, mounted on the wall would work well. Remember, people seeing the actual OOH when in place will most likely be reviewing it at speed. They will not have an ample amount of time to scrutinize every element of the design. Keep that in mind as the people critiquing begin to discuss things like the amount of copy on the board (of lack thereof).

## Broadcast or Web

It only makes sense that elements created for use on TV (TV spots) or on the Web (websites, digital banners) should be reviewed on a TV or a monitor, right? The bright, vibrant colors selected and used on broadcast or the Web can't be adequately displayed in all of their vibrancy because print dulls down the colors. Be sure that if any work is being created to be consumed by your target audience in the digital realm, it should be reviewed digitally.

## What Kind of Room Should You Use?

The size of the room in which you hold your critique session isn't as important as access to a whiteboard or something to write on. You'll want to utilize a room where you can minimize distractions and keep everyone focused. Ideally you'll also have a television monitor so you can project the digital or TV work for everyone to review at once. If not, you should at least have a laptop available to use as a display.

## In a Nutshell

Critiques can be fun or they can be painful. Some agencies or design studios don't call them critiques. They simply call meetings to go over concepts. Call them whatever you want, it really doesn't matter. What does matter is that you have them. If you have a team who communicates well critiques might happen anywhere—from the hallway to the break room to the coffee shop. Critiques are key to being able to benchmark the progress of your team's creative development. Evaluating your team's creative work is a routine part of your process that will lead to positive results only for your team, but also for your clients and your company.

# The Art of the Pitch

## Get ready for the spotlight.

Coming up with good ideas is hard enough, but convincing others that they are good is a whole other ballgame. Part of the responsibility of being creative lead is that it is your job to present or "pitch" ideas to both internal team members and clients. I am not advocating that you learn how to sell ideas like one of those slick car wheeler-dealers, but you do need to thoroughly communicate the benefits of your creative solutions to teammates and the clients. You must develop the ability to be at ease when speaking to a group of people so that you can present your team's ideas in a confident, knowledgeable manner. If you can't, you risk having very good ideas end up in the recycle bin.

Ah, the pitch. We live and die by the pitch. If you are or want to be a creative lead and aren't comfortable doing pitches, you will not go far. The most successful creative directors (CDs) pitch ideas often and they do it well. If you can't sell your ideas or your vision, how will you ever advance? Sadly, many people's vision or experience with pitching comes from watching episodes of AMC's *Mad Men*. In between the womanizing, excessive drinking, smoking, and rampant sexuality depicted on the show, there are moments showing the creatives pitching ideas to clients and each other. We—executive CDs, CDs, associate CDs… or whatever title you hold—constantly sell our ideas.

© Eleazar Hernández 2017
E. Hernández, *Leading Creative Teams*, DOI 10.1007/978-1-4842-2056-6_8

Whether you like to do it or not, pitching is part of the gig, my friends. You know the work better than anyone else, and nobody is more invested in it than you. So you are the best person to pitch the ideas and convince others of its merits. Without the pitch to secure approvals, there is no work. No work means no money. No money means lots of Top Ramen and Kool-Aid for dinner.

Like all things in our journey to being the best creative lead you can be, there are good ways and bad ways to pitch. I will go over them here. Before beginning, I do want to stress that you don't have to be an extrovert all the time to excel at pitching. You only have to be great when you're pitching. If you recede into the background and shy away from opportunities to get up in front of a crowd to pitch ideas or give presentations you will soon find creatives who are willing to get up in front of people, surpassing you on your journey.

If you're shy, suck it up playa. Be shy when you're alone. Creative leads are the biggest personalities in the room. They are willing to go out on a ledge and throw ideas out that other people might be afraid to share. They willingly get up and speak to groups. The good news is that this is something you can learn. The bad news is that the only way to get better at pitching is to pitch. You'll have to overcome your fear, anxiety, or insecurities. Pitching is a skill just like any other. The more you do it, the better you'll get at it.

Although fields or industries may differ (advertising, graphic design, media buying, web design, public relations, etc.), the basic ideas behind pitching are largely the same.

Think you can you do this? Is it something you want to do? Then read on. Let's go.

# Selling Creative Ideas

So what do you need to know before you pitch your idea? You need to understand who you're pitching to. If you know who your audience is you can tailor your message and the way you present it so you have a much greater chance of success.

Let's assume that you've brainstormed ideas, you've gone through rounds of revisions with your creative team, and now you're ready to share them. The first group you'll have to convince of your idea's ability to address your client's challenges is your Account Service team. They will judge your solutions against the creative brief that was provided when your team was assigned the job. Although this is an internal checkpoint and you don't necessarily need completely fleshed-out creative work, it should at least be at a stage that your Account Service team can review and understand the solutions.

Why flesh out your ideas for the first checkpoint presentation? Because people can poke holes through an idea that is interesting but vague. Some people have a hard time visualizing ideas. If they have tangible creative concepts to review it's much more difficult to dismiss.

Always remember, moving from an interesting but vague idea to specific and actionable is the difficult part of the creative process.

Most of the time it's not worth pitching an idea until you're able to answer some pragmatic questions about it: What problem does this solve? What evidence is there that the problem is real and important enough to solve—or in the corporate world, solve profitably? What are the toughest logistical challenges when executing the idea and how will (or would) you solve them? Do you have a prototype, sample, or demonstration of an implementation of the idea (a.k.a. proof of concept)? Why should this problem be solved now? Why should our organization be the one selected to solve this problem? These are the kinds of questions you are likely to be asked, and therefore, you'll need to be prepared.

# Prepping for the Pitch

Before going into the lion's den, you want to know as much as you can about your client. You must have a solid understanding of who your client is as well as who their target market is. By doing so, you can almost predict what types of questions or concerns they will have with the creative work that you are about to present to them. By getting a firm understanding of who they are, where they've been, and what they've done in the past, you and your team can develop strategies demonstrating not only that you understand them, but that you and your team have come up with solutions that meet or exceed their needs.

Your clients are willing to spend money on your ideas, but they will only do so if they feel they can trust you. As the creative lead, you are going in with ideas that may be contrary to what they've done in the past. If you go in without any reference as to why you're doing what you're doing and putting it in terms they understand or are willing to accept, you may be in for a challenge.

I am not saying that by understanding their history and speaking their language your pitches will always be successful. What I am saying is you need to understand your client's personality. How far will they let you take things? Do they enjoy humor? Are they really into technology? Do they like bright colors or do they like neutral color palettes? You've got to know these things to make your pitch much more likely to be a successful one.

# Three Ways to Pitch Ideas

There are three approaches to pitching ideas: extemporaneous, keywords, and rehearsed. Each approach has its good and bad points. As you read through this you may find that one seems to be more appealing to you than the other two. What I recommend is you find the approach that best suits your style and go with it.

## Extemporaneous presentations

Believe it or not, in the past I rarely ever have really been one to rehearse for a presentation. Whether I was the creative lead at an agency or working on my own, when it was time to pitch ideas I typically studied the challenges faced by the client, reviewed what my solutions were, and then headed off to pitch my ideas. I was always able to hit the main points of the solution while addressing the client's challenges. While that is not the best solution for presenting ideas, it worked for me at the time. You probably don't want to try this approach if you have a tendency to forget information when you get nervous. We are all nervous when we present, so if this is a serious problem for you avoid extemporaneous presentations at all costs. In hindsight, I see how lucky I was to be able to pull off this way of presenting. I was at risk of not providing key insights that could make the difference between winning and not winning accounts.

## Keyword presentations

If extemporaneous pitches aren't your style, you can try using keywords. You don't want to memorize a speech because reciting a speech from memory gives it a canned quality and distances a speaker from his or her listeners. There is also the risk of losing track of where you are in the speech if something distracts you while you speak. Writing down a list of keywords or phrases on an index card or piece of paper works well. While I really dislike having anything in my hands when I am presenting, a small document with keywords helps to remind me to talk about the most important aspects of items I am presenting. When you use keywords on an index card, you are less likely to forget something important.

## Rehearsed presentations

Rehearsing for presentations is a very effective way to get ready for a pitch. When I worked at GDC Marketing + Ideation, I saw the benefit of rehearsing for pitches firsthand. The team—Frank Guerra, Beth Wammack, Carey Quackenbush, Victor Noriega, Lisa Gomez, and Marcie Casas—worked very hard at their presentation skills. Each member of the pitch team practiced their respective portions of the pitch (creative, media, public relations, etc.) and then they came together as a unit to rehearse multiple times before presenting ideas to current and potential clients. They did not try to memorize their presentations. They rehearsed multiple times so their presentations would appear effortless. It worked.

Following my time working with the GDC team, being able to watch their process firsthand, I am a firm proponent of every creative lead rehearsing their presentations before they sell ideas to clients. Rehearsing (not memorizing) will help you become more comfortable and confident with the delivery of your message once you are standing in front of your audience.

# Hello My Name Is...

Be sure to mingle before a large presentation so you have an opportunity to learn who is going to be listening to your pitch. Once you get their names, write them down and try to remember them so you can refer to audience members by name during the pitch or when it's time for Q and A.

What's even better? When people walk into the room where the pitch is going to happen, shake hands, introduce yourself, and then get their names so you can make a quick seating chart. You can use this seating chart to write down anything that you might want to reference during your presentation or after. Try to be sly about it. Don't look at the seating chart you made and use a person's name at the same time. Refer to your seating chart, speak for 5 to 10 seconds, and then refer to them by name.

By using their names, you are showing that you care enough to learn who they are. You are also building rapport and will grab their attention. In addition, doing this can help stop distracting conversations between audience members.

# Engage the Audience

For those who have already had an opportunity to pitch ideas, have you ever pitched to a person or group of people who had no reaction or seemed bored? Pitching to a reactionless audience is somewhat painful. You will have a higher likelihood of either winning new business or getting a client to approve your campaign approach by engaging with them during your pitch. You need to get them to react. If you can break the ice and make a connection with them, they will feel comfortable enough to ask questions or make comments during your pitch. Once this happens, you have changed the dynamic of the pitch from a one-way presentation to a two-way discussion.

Some presenters get flustered by clients interrupting their pitches because they believe it messes up their flow. This is one of the main reasons that I now believe that prior preparation of the presentation is key. If you practice, you will be able to get back on track should you be interrupted in midthought.

Many presenters dislike interruptions because they don't see it as a beneficial course of action. Interruptions aren't always bad. If the interruption signals that the client is agreeing with your ideas or contributing to what you're saying, then the interruption is a very good thing. When you are able to converse with clients during the pitch, when there is an open exchange of ideas and information, the atmosphere can change to something more informative and (hopefully) successful.

When the pitch is going well and turns into a conversation, the conversation can sometimes turn into a mini-workshop. What I mean by a mini-workshop is that the client or potential client is so engaged with your ideas that now they have moved from merely being the recipient of the pitch to engaging with and helping to move the idea of your pitch forward. They will begin to see the ideas as actionable items that can be used to spread their message out to their target audience. Pitching to an engaged client is not just more enjoyable for you; the client will also feel as if they get more out of the meeting.

How do you engage with your audience? What has always worked for me is removing any physical barriers between me and them. If there is a lectern step out from behind it and move closer to your audience. Proximity helps to make a more personal connection with them. If you are in a large room with a long rectangular conference table, more often than not there are people at the table whose view is being blocked by someone else's big ol' cabeza. Give everyone the attention they deserve by moving around the room so they all feel equally engaged and equally important.

## Pacing Your Presentation

I believe that everyone has their own presentation style. Believe it or not, I used to be a deacon at First Baptist Church in upstate New York. Yup, it's true. During my tenure there, I asked the pastor about presentation styles to try and understand how certain sermons seemed to get people excited. From church to church, I noticed that some congregations were super-engaged while others were more subdued. I asked if it was the content of the sermon or the way in which it was presented. The pastor informed me that the reaction from the congregation can be a direct correlation to the presentation style of the person giving the sermon.

That's when I learned about the presentation technique church leaders are taught in seminary to get their congregations engaged and energized during their sermons. The method was broken down into four phases:

- Start low
- Go slow
- Raise higher
- Catch fire

Through the years, I have adapted that method to my presentation style. While I am not asking people to jump up and down shouting, "Yes Eli! I agree! That is the best idea I've ever heard! We should all buy two large pizzas with up to five toppings each for $20! You are as clever as you are artistically gifted! Amen! Amen! Amen!"

Okay, well that would be kinda funny. In reality, I provide initial information and build to my main points. I also adjust my pace and intensity according to what I'm presenting, or how important a certain aspect of the presentation is.

I also try to inject a bit of personality into my presentations. As a Puerto Rican, native New Yorker, I have a certain way of speaking. There is some Spanglish here and there, along with a bit of humor. Honestly I don't plan for anything funny to be said, it just kind of hits me at the moment, and it seems to work for me.

Another thing I do is ensure that there is positive energy in the meeting. I am enthusiastic about the ideas I am pitching, but it is a measured enthusiasm. Overenthusiasm can make you come off as fake and insincere. You will find that measured, sincere enthusiasm in your pitches might make your clients keener to accept your concepts and design advice than a pitch that lacks enthusiasm or seems insincere.

## Setting the Stage

Don't jump right into the work without reminding your client why you're pitching to them in the first place. Set up the situation or the marketing challenge that got you in front of them. Do it accurately and succinctly. You've got a very short amount of time at the beginning of the pitch to set up your ideas and get your client in the right mindset to receive your ideas. When you begin, they are already making decisions about you. Typically people make positive or negative judgments quickly and you'll either be in for smooth sailing or a battle for survival.

Make sure that you make a good first impression. I am somewhat casual in the way I like to dress. I love to wear a great pair of jeans with some nice shoes, a sport coat, and a nicely colored shirt to presentations. I believe if you're comfortable when you're pitching ideas, your presentation will be great. However, if you are presenting to a very uptight dress code—oriented organization, you'll want to dress in the manner in which *they* feel is appropriate.

## Build Trust

You can build trust with your clients by giving them three things: honesty, ability, and concern.

- Honesty—Clients value people who tell them the truth. They want straight talk. Don't beat around the bush.

- Ability—Clients want to know you can do your job. Don't pitch an idea for something you have absolutely no idea how to turn into reality. Don't promise things you can't deliver.

- Concern—Clients need to know you're on their side. Feeling that you are providing solutions that are in their best interest is probably the single largest concern that clients have with agencies. If they don't trust you, your relationship will not last very long.

# The Target Audience

Understanding your target audience is critical. If you don't understand your target, how can you convince your account team that your creative solution is valid? If your concepts don't resonate with the target, how will you get the client's green light to produce the work? When you're presenting your ideas, you will need to justify why your ideas will reach the target. Some of the questions you should be able to answer are as follows:

- What is the primary way in which the target receives information? Print? Web? Social Media? Word of mouth?

- How much time does the target spend on these mediums?

- How does your solution reach the target?

- Why does your solution specifically resonate with the target?

- Is your solution true to the brand?

Consider this: it is important to show the client how the target audience will view their marketing messages. If you are pitching an advertising campaign for your client, you should show your idea of the way the target audience will view the ad. If you have print collateral (brochures, postcards, flyers, etc.), the best way to show the elements is to print them full-size so the client can see the pieces and examine them the way the target audience will. Are you pitching a digital ad campaign? Don't go in with only printed examples of your digital ads to get approval. Show them how your ads will look onscreen whether it's on a laptop or iPad. Digital ads are much brighter onscreen than when they get printed out. Do you have an out-of-home campaign you'd like to pitch? Some media companies actually have mini billboard mock-ups you can use for your pitch.

What exactly am I trying to get at here? Pay attention to how you are planning to solve a client's marketing challenge. Be sure that you utilize the best possible method to show your work so they understand how it will be received by the target audience. Take your target audience into account and understand the best way to reach them with your information. Millennial targets optimally receive information differently than Boomers, for instance.

# ¿Me entiendes?

While we typically deal with visual ways to pitch ideas to clients, people have different ways of processing information: visual, auditory, or kinesthetic. Without the benefit of knowing how the people on the client side will receive your work best, you will need to be prepared to address each modality. What are the best ways to cater to the different modalities?

- **Visual modality**—drawings, charts, photos, videos, graphs, and so on.

- **Auditory modality**—wordplay, verbal emphasis, stats, facts, emotions, verbal pauses, cadence, tone, and so on.

- **Kinesthetic modality**—textures, props, handouts, models, and so on.

Now that you've addressed the manners in which your clients will receive your pitch, you need to sell the work. What you want to do is paint a picture for your client and get them to buy in.

# Now it's Time for the Spotlight

This is where you can differentiate yourself from other creatives. Good creatives can create. Great creatives can not only create, but they can also sell. If you can stand in front of a client and present ideas that get them excited and ultimately encourage them to hire your team, then you'll go far. Some of the ideas and techniques are the same whether you are pitching an integrated branding campaign for a multimillion dollar company or an identity campaign for a smaller company. Let's look at some of the things you should be aware of.

## Be happy. Smile. Make eye contact.

There is nothing more engaging than a person who is smiling while they speak to you. Now I'm not talking about a big, toothy shark grin, I am speaking about a genuine "I'm happy to be here presenting the ideas to you" smile. You should be pleased and honored to have these people give you their time. Show it with an engaging smile. The smile you display will also help them understand that you are not only happy about presenting work, but at least you are also confident that you are providing them with the best solutions possible.

When you smile, it will help to decrease your own tension and creates a warm environment. A smile tells people, "I am prepared for this and I will make this an interesting and informative presentation for you." If you appear relaxed, your audience will also relax.

Eye contact is also important. Look at the people you are speaking to. Engage with them visually, but don't stare at them... that's just creepy. Glance around the room. Look at your team for their agreement and support. Look at your clients, each one of them. Don't look at the same people in the same pattern repeatedly. That'll just make you look like a water sprinkler. Visually jump from person to person in random patterns. Break down the room from groups to individuals. Each person you're speaking to should feel as if they are the only person in the room. Make a connection with the people you are presenting to. Change the dynamic from a presentation to a chat between friends.

A typical mistake made in pitches is for the presenter to look exclusively at the person they believe is the decision-maker. Bad move playa. If you do this, you will alienate the other people in the room. You are pretty much telling everyone besides the decision-maker, "You're not important." If you alienate people on the receiving end of your presentation, they won't have positive things to say about you and they may decide they don't like what you were presenting to them. Their opinions will likely have an impact on the final decision. You want everyone in the room to advocate on your behalf.

# Body posture

Talking through your ideas is only one part of the equation. You have to be very cognizant of your body posture as well. The way you stand, the way you move, the way you emphasize key points: all of these send messages. Your audience can read you as uptight or nonchalant, timid or challenging, sheepish or restrained. Avoid distracting movements or lack of movements, and for goodness sake don't ever have a clickable pen or a snap-top marker in your hand: you'll click your audience to death!

You will find that there are typically three types of presentation setups that you'll be faced with: seated, standing, and lectern. Here are some tips for all three methods of presenting.

## Seated presentation

Although they are not ideal for presentations, seated presentations work best for small meetings or in small rooms. It's a little disconcerting to stand over your client in a very small room to present your work to them. While I would rather be in a large room to present, smaller rooms can make an event feel a little more intimate. In these scenarios, remember:

- Be comfortable, but don't be lazy. Don't slouch into your chair.

- Leaning slightly forward toward the person you're speaking to will add energy to your delivery. You will be perceived as having enthusiasm for what you're presenting.

- Square your shoulders to the person with whom you are conversing during the presentation. Don't merely move your head from side to side. Squaring up your shoulders to everyone you speak to invites them into the presentation.

- When squaring up your shoulders to different people at the table, don't swivel your chair from side to side. Randomly square up to different people and establish eye contact.

- When presenting to a crowd, square your shoulders up to different parts of the room.

## Standing presentation

When you're presenting in large conference rooms or theaters, standing is the way to go. There is something about standing up in front of a group that immediately gets your audience's attention and helps you get your message across. To help things go your way while standing, try these tips:

- Do not pace from side to side in a repetitive pattern. It's very distracting and makes you appear anxious.

- Do not shift your weight from one foot to another. It makes you seem extremely unconfident.

- Keep your hands moving naturally as you speak. Use them to gesture and emphasize your points. Try not to clasp your hands together or lock your fingers.

- Try to avoid fidgety hands. Fidgety hands make you appear nervous or uncomfortable with the topic.

- Do not lock your elbows to your sides. Relax; let your arms move freely.

- Make eye contact with all parts of the room. Don't just focus on one or two people.

- Stand tall.

## Presenting from a lectern

Lecterns are common in classrooms, as well as some conference rooms and large venues like theaters. All tips from standing presentations apply here, and in addition:

- Do not lean in or touch your stomach to the lectern. If you do, you risk knocking your notes down or shifting your view down to the lectern thus not looking at your audience.

- Stand tall to ensure that you don't get lost behind the lectern.

- Resist the urge to place your hands on the lectern. If you must, rest them on the lectern, but do not have a death grip on the edges.

- Don't lean over the lectern or rest any part of your body on the lectern, it'll make you appear lazy or nonchalant.

---

**Don't Turn Your Back to Your Audience!** This tip is so important that it should be highlighted. In my opinion, turning your back to your audience to read your slide is horribly disrespectful to your audience. Not only do you begin to speak to the slide, it also implies that you don't know what you're presenting because you have to look at your slides for information. As creative lead, you should know everything about the slides that are being projected. If anything, you should be able to quickly glance at the visual and then explain it in its entirety to the audience. When you turn your back to your audience, you lose credibility very quickly.

---

# Work the Room

As any good performer will tell you, you need to work the room to ensure that you connect with the audience and they respond favorably to you. How do you do this when you're presenting? You must be able to adjust your pacing to keep the audience engaged throughout your pitch. In some cases you can even adjust some of the details of your pitch based on the verbal and non-verbal cues that your client is sending your way. This is critical to the success of your pitches. Your goal is not only to show the ideas you have developed, but to explain how they will benefit your client. Three quick tips to help you work the room:

- Don't beat around the bush.

- Speak clearly.

- Give them the information and pause for a minute to let them absorb it.

# Don't be a Cocky Jerk

Whatever you do, don't jump into a pitch and act like a slick car salesperson. Additionally, don't go into a pitch as the chuckling, sycophantic, promise-the-world schmuck. You'll lose a client's trust and confidence immediately. Be honest. Be engaging. Your audience is smart. They will see through any insincere behavior.

# Take Small Bites, Giuseppe!

Have you ever tried to shove an entire foot-long sandwich into your mouth all at once? No? If you were to try, do you think you could ingest it in one gulp? Think of your campaign presentation as a foot-long sandwich. Don't try to shove an entire campaign down your client's gullet. Break your concept into pieces. Gradually present the pieces and let them build to make the whole. It'll be a lot easier for them to swallow.

For example, say you and your team are tasked with providing a new branding campaign for a local credit union. This assignment asks you to consider a complete shift in the way the brand is displayed to the public because the client has done some advertising that really hasn't helped them stand out in a crowded marketplace. You and your team work up a new brand voice that includes headlines and impactful, informative copy. You've worked on defining new visual vocabulary with unique imagery, you've selected secondary colors to support the brand color palette, and you've generated ideas for the creation of print and digital ads, collateral materials, and internal publications. What you're about to pitch is a solution that moves the client's messaging away from anything else in the marketplace. Because the solution is such a broad shift, when it's time to pitch the ideas to the client it would be best to unveil a little at a time. Give them a roadmap to follow that leads them through the details and ends up with the final, cohesive solution.

So let's put this situation in terms of starting low, going slow, raising higher, catching fire:

- **Starting low**—Give an introduction that explains why you are there, what you believe your assignment required, and how you plan to progress through the pitch.

- **Going slow**—Begin to unveil the different elements. Start with the new visuals to show how you will evolve the photo treatments and subjects of their communications. Next, go over the headlines to show how the words will get people's attention while supporting and being supported by the imagery. Next, explain the personality that will be exuded in the body copy. Finally, show how the secondary color palette supports the primary brand colors and explain how they should elicit certain responses.

- **Raising higher**—Show how the elements work together. How will horizontal and vertical print advertisements look? Give them an idea how digital advertisements will get attention on web pages. Showcase how out-of-home messaging could be succinct yet informative.

- **Catching fire**—Now's your chance to get them really excited by showing them how the elements come together for the public. Create mock-ups of the different communications solutions in context. Show a print ad in a newspaper or magazine being read by someone. Place a digital ad on a web page that shows how it looks in context. Show how the billboards would look when viewed by a person driving by in a vehicle. How will their new elements appear on an iPhone?

## So a Designer and a Copywriter Walk into a Bar...

Utilizing humor in your pitches is one way to break down barriers and make a connection with the people to whom you are pitching because it's difficult to disagree with someone you're laughing with. Humor can be used to your advantage; however, be very careful. Not everyone has the ability to pull off a joke during a presentation. If you can't joke successfully, don't try to use humor during your pitches. It could make things really uncomfortable when it flops. Believe me, when a joke flops it's difficult to get back on track.

If you want to play it safe, try using a relevant funny story or analogy in your presentation. It's easier to tell a story than to tell a joke. If they don't laugh at your story, at least you've delivered your message.

Keep your eyes open to the world around you. There's humor everywhere from books to magazines, TV to the web. Find things that are humorous and see how to incorporate them, but always be aware who is in your audience. Not everyone will find some things humorous.

## Defend Your Work

Part of the job of a CD is not only to show the work, but to defend it from people who may not agree with it. You need to be confident in your position that your work is not only strategic but addresses the client's marketing challenge and speaks to the target demographic. You will sometimes be faced by coworkers as well as clients who will give the "I don't like it" response even though they are not in the target demographic. It's only natural for people to view things in their own terms and based on their own experiences. To combat this, you *must* make sure that you have research about the target demographic so you can defend your work in terms of data and information rather than anyone's (including your own) personal likes or dislikes.

It's frustrating to create a campaign targeted to a Millennial-aged audience and hear a Baby Boomer client say they don't "like" it because they don't understand it. If you have research to back up why your team's work is solid, then you will have a stronger position to defend. You will have numbers, case studies, testimonials, and articles to support your work. Maybe you'll win the battle. Maybe you won't, but at least you'll know you had the support of research to back up your creative decisions and you did your best to provide enough information to support your team's creative solution.

## Caveat: Don't Ever Show Crap Work

Whatever you do, if you don't like the work, don't show it. I have been hurt by this idea more than once. I was asked to show something I was not 100% convinced was the best solution, but unfortunately that's what the client chose. It sucks to show work that you don't believe in, have it approved by the client, and then have to execute it knowing that another idea could have been more successful. To avoid this, only show work you are convinced is the best solution *and* that you and your team will be happy and proud to produce.

## Life and Death by the Deck

As a creative, I have to say I absolutely hate horrible-looking presentations. Presentations full of lame clip art, drop shadows, flashing words, flipping photos… ugh! Pretty much all the cutesy stuff that can be done with PowerPoint or Keynote, I really dislike. If I attend a presentation and the presenter has a horribly designed slide presentation, I'll have a difficult time paying attention to what they are saying. I am not able to get past their distracting slides. Slides deserve quite a bit of attention because they will be onscreen while you are speaking. You must take the necessary time to create good ones or you risk losing a good percentage of your audience before you get to the main point of your pitch. Visuals can add to what you're saying just as quickly as they can detract from it. So what's the point here? I recommend a KISS strategy (Keep It Simple Shiboink). Let me give you quick tips for improving presentations.

## We Are Visual Creatures

It's imperative that you think about how imagery can enhance your message. Don't rely on PowerPoint or Keynote transitions or visual treatments to enhance your message. You want your audience to have an emotional response to your visuals. Here are some quick tips:

- Don't place everything in the center of the slide. Try using the rule of thirds. Imagine your screen is divided vertically and horizontally into thirds. Place the focal point of your image where the horizontal and vertical lines would intersect.

- Blur out distracting elements (busy background patterns, unnecessary people, random objects, etc.) from any photography.

- Check stock photo sites for visuals, but be very selective about what you use. Stock photos can help, or they can just be lame. How many times do we have to see business people with their arms crossed looking at the camera with an intense, but determined gaze? Oh barf! Don't just grab the first image you see. Use some imagination. Never use images with logo watermarks on them.

- Use colors to elicit certain responses. (blue=calm, red=passion, yellow=sun, orange=energy, etc.)

- Use dark text on a light background because it's easier to read, but avoid stark white backgrounds because in a dark room a stark white background is somewhat blinding.

- Don't use custom or kitschy fonts they are distracting and sometimes difficult to read

- Keep text large and use minimal bullets per slide because people will naturally try to read what you place on a slide. If there are too many bullets with lots of copy, your audience will stop listening to you and begin to read your bullets.

- Avoid long sentences because you and your audience will read them. Presenters who read their slides lose credibility quickly. If you have too much text on your slides, you may be tempted to read them verbatim. Opt instead for keywords because keywords are easier to remember.

- Keep your focus to only two to five points per slide max. This helps keep you from lingering on a slide too long.

- As you create your slides, constantly organize them and refine your flow (Slide Sorter view in PowerPoint or Light Table view in Keynote). Remember start low, go slow, raise higher, and catch fire.

- If a slide doesn't work, get rid of it.

# Write for Brevity

Imagine you're writing for Twitter. Try to keep your phrases to a minimal number of words. Strive for words that are conversational yet impactful. However, don't pare down important words. Don't sacrifice clarity for brevity.

Consider two versions of a slide bullet:

Too Wordy:

- It is believed that the fall of the Roman Empire affected coin-operated lint-picking machines by positively increasing their use among Roman citizens by 25 percent.

Better:

- After the fall of the Roman Empire, coin-operated lint-picking machines usage increased 25 percent.

## Always Keep Your Audience Guessing

Follow up keyword-heavy slides with slides containing a single, large image or large field of color with minimal copy. This will keep your audience from getting bored with your layout. Adding variety will also help keep them engaged. Throw in a joke or maybe a photo of your favorite pet to see if they are paying attention. You can also consider adding variety to the slides by introducing charts, images, illustrations, quotes, and so on.

# To Comp or Not to Comp? That is the Question

There some situations where you pitch to those few gifted clients who have the eye; the people that can see and understand what you're pitching by merely looking at a sketch. Then there are others who are very literal. They need to see everything in detail. Or maybe it's not them; maybe you're presenting an idea that can really only be appreciated when the client can see how it will look when it's executed. You will have to understand in what form you ideas must be presented when it's time to pitch them to your client.

I'm not saying that you have to spend $500 on a photo in an effort to secure approval from your client. You can have your team do all kinds of things. If you have an ad idea that requires a certain arrangement of people, you've got an agency full of models to choose from. Select people from your creative team, your media, account service, and public relations team and stage the photo you need. You don't have a camera? Sure you do. You've got an iPhone or other smart phone that can take photos. Want to show them how the work will look on a billboard, a bus, or stenciled on the sidewalk? You've got a creative team who can take the photos you need and mock it up in Photoshop or you can utilize any free mock-up site online to get images you can use in your pitch. The only limit you have is your own imagination.

You are selling ideas. To sell them you need to make sure the person who is buying them can imagine what you're seeing. You can display the power of your ideas with mock-ups that show how they will actually look to the public in context.

## Handouts Before the Pitch? Just Say "No!"

Whatever you do, don't hand out material before you pitch your ideas. As soon as you give a client something to look at, you are competing with your own material for their attention. They will flip through it and inevitably steal your thunder by trying to get to the meat of your presentation.

If you want to provide the clients with handouts, let them know you will do so after your presentation. That way they have something to refer to or even jot notes on once you are finished.

## A Roadmap for You to Follow

Pitching creative work is best done in a systematic way. If you are able to present to clients in a way that makes it easy for them to imagine the work and digest the different elements, you will hook them and be that much closer to an approval. You shouldn't make a presentation confusing for a client and expect a positive outcome. If they get confused they will most likely not approve anything.

For example, the way in which storyboards are presented to clients can cause quite a bit of confusion. Because storyboards are typically designed with the visual description on the left side of the page, the visuals in the center, and the audio or dialogue on the right side of the page, some creative leaders present the boards in a left-to-right, top-to-bottom manner (Figure 8-1).

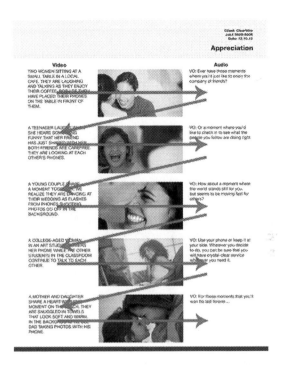

**Figure 8-1.** An example of bad narrative flow in a storyboard presentation

In other words, the creative reads the description of slide 1, shows the visual, then reads the dialogue or voice-over for slide 1. Then on to presenting slide 2 in the same manner and so on, and so on. In my opinion, that is one of the worst ways to present a TV concept to a client. This manner of presenting a storyboard doesn't allow for the client to imagine the visuals of the spot before they are trying to absorb the audio. It breaks up the flow of the dialogue because the presenter is always describing the scene while the client is still digesting the narrative.

I believe there is a much better way to present: a presentation road map. Not only is the following road map a good way to present TV ideas, it can be used for most other creative presentations. There are two aspects to the presentation road map: the presentation of the storyboard and the presentation of the ideas. If you follow this roadmap to pitch your ideas, you will find that your clients are able to engage with and absorb the information being presented to them much quicker.

First, try organizing your ideas like this:

1. **Objective**—what are you trying to accomplish?
2. **Target**
    1. *Demographic*—the structure of populations.
    2. *Psychographic*—the study and classification of people according to their attitudes, aspirations, and other psychological criteria, especially in market research.
    3. *Brand, product, or service benefit*—why does the audience care?
3. **Challenge**—what is the opportunity available to educate the public? What is the obstacle that must be overcome?
4. **Concept**—present the idea in a way that excites the client.
5. **Wrap-up**—a single sentence set up to provide context for what you're about to show.
6. **Execution**—show work.

Second, when you present the storyboard, rather than describing the visuals then reading the audio portion and jumping back to the visuals for the next frame and its associated audio, and so on and so on, try something different. Provide the client with the visuals. Describe each frame and set up the tone of the spot (Figure 8-2). As you progress through your PowerPoint (or Keynote) presentation you can give the client the details of the scene. You can sing or hum the song that will be playing in the background. You can even mimic some of the movements of the actors in the spot.

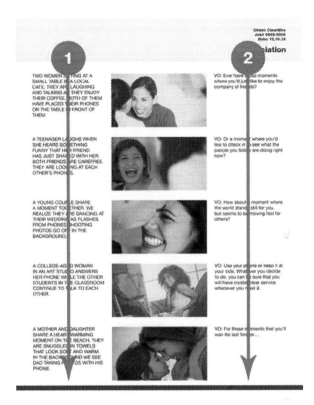

**Figure 8-2.** Present the visual first then go over the audio portion.

Once you finish with the visuals, the presentation will go back to the first frame and you can read through the audio portion of the spot. Whether it's the talent speaking or a voice-over, you can walk the client through the spot one more time. Now that the client has seen the visuals and been provided with your description, the audio portion will make more of a connection.

---

**Note** When you're pitching TV storyboard ideas, try to avoid using technical camera jargon. Keep your verbiage simple and concise so it's easy to understand. You are presenting the overall idea; you don't need to go into the minutia such as camera movements, coloring, or effects… yet.

---

Now, let's take a look at how all this can work.

# Case Study

Let's take an imaginary journey into a creative pitch for a TV spot. The client is a latex condom company. Their goal is to get people to always use condoms so they can avoid any diseases or unwanted pregnancies. I will provide the pitch dialogue after which in parenthesis I explain what portion of the roadmap I have just provided.

CD: Good morning everyone. Our team is here to present a concept for a TV spot that will run during the Super Bowl. As we all know, TV spots during the Super Bowl are a great way to showcase your product in a way that will not only engage and entertain, but will reach millions of people. With this in mind, we understand that our main objective is to sell more condoms. (**Objective**—*First, you set up the presentation by giving information about the purpose of the meeting then tell them what you understand is their marketing challenge.*)

CD: We know that we are reaching a vast audience during the Super Bowl, but our main target are those very eager young men 18 to 24 years old who may not be thinking clearly enough to consider buying a condom before engaging in sexual relations. We are trying to get them to take control of their lives before their lives take control of them. In addition, we are reminding our target that they are not only being responsible for themselves, they are also behaving responsibly for their partner. (**Target**—*The client is being told who the target audience is, what the target audience has in mind, and why the target should care.*)

CD: Our goal with this spot is to show not only that your product is the best in terms of sensitivity, but that it is THE safest condom on the market because it is very strong. (**Challenge**—*Outline what the challenge is and what you expect the target will get from your creative idea.*)

CD: How strong are your condoms? You condoms are SO STRONG they can stop almost anything. (**Concept**—*Give the client a description of the spot that hints to the type of solution you will be presenting. In this case it's an exaggeration.*)

CD: Because sperm, like petulant children, need to be controlled. (**Wrap-Up**—*Sum up the spot with a simple statement.*)

CD: Before I begin, allow me to play a small snippet of music that will help set the mood: the song "Feelings" by Morris Albert. (Play the song and begin to describe the images of the spot.) We see a young man walking down a typical street. He is obviously dressed to go out on a date. Behind him we see thousands of men dressed in round, white costumes with pointy white hats. The oddly dressed men—who look surprisingly similar to a certain male reproductive cell—mimic every move the young man makes. When the young man walks faster, they walk faster. When the young man stops to look at his watch, they stop to look at their watches. When the young man stops to look at himself in the window of a sexy lingerie store, they stop, look at themselves and get very excited. Finally the young man has reached his destination. He stops and waves to someone in the distance. We see his girlfriend. She waves back at him from across the street.

CD (suddenly stop the music that has been playing): The young man begins to fix his collar and prepares to step off the curb toward his girlfriend. Without warning, he is run over by the thousands of chubby white sperm men! They charge toward the girlfriend. Thousands of sperm men are running toward her. As these men charge, the girlfriend's expression changes from happy to concerned. Suddenly, the men run into an invisible barrier just before they reach her.

CD: The young man walks up to his girlfriend and takes her by the arm, and they walk off into the night together. As they walk away, they pass the world's largest condom filled with the thousands of sperm men who were following the young man all night. We conclude by watching the sperm men struggling in vain to get past the barrier.

CD: As we see the sperm men struggling, your logo appears with a simple line that reads: For a hundred million reasons. (**Execution**—*First, provide a visual description of the spot only showing images from the frames of your storyboard. In this case there is not any voice-over or dialogue, but if there were, you could go through the storyboard images once more, and read the dialogue the second time. Doing it this way allows your client to first see the images and enjoy them before listening to what the audio portion will be.)*

# In a Nutshell

There you have it. Easy. Right? Of course not. If it were really easy then everyone could do it.

Pitching is a skill that must be learned and practiced. It is a way to present the benefits of a communications strategy that you and your team have developed. Pitching is something that CDs must continually do and do well. They pitch to their account team to get approvals to move forward with ideas; they pitch to clients to get their approvals to execute their ideas; and they pitch to potential clients to get their business and sign them on as clients.

When you're pitching ideas you must take everything into consideration from researching your client to understanding how they will most likely react to your presentation to the ideas you present and the way you present them. If you're currently on your way up the career ladder working toward a CD position and you have an opportunity to present ideas to the account team, to a client, to your creative team, to anyone, *do it*. The only way to get better pitching ideas is to do it and do it frequently.

Remember, for a CD: Life's a pitch.

# The Art of Copywriting

## Writing copy for an overstimulated world

What is copywriting? Simply put, you can think of it as salesmanship in written form. It is used for the purpose of relaying a client's advertising or marketing message. Great copywriting has the ability to deliver messages of value to the right people at the right time. Effective messaging will motivate readers to respond with thoughts, words, or actions. If they are not motivated to act or at least consider taking action, the copy was not successful. You may be thinking, "Yeah. Sure. Whatever. That's easy. It's just words." Don't underestimate the power of good copywriting.

Copywriting is not just about writing; it's also about the strategy behind the writing. With a strategically sound writing plan, you can convince people to take action—buy a new hamburger, vote, care about a cause, you name it. If you have a specific outcome in mind, copy is part of the creative mixture that can help deliver it.

Copywriting is about tone, as well. How do you want readers to imagine the sound of the messaging in their heads? Do they hear a happy voice or an authoritative voice? Is the message humorous or serious?

© Eleazar Hernández 2017
E. Hernández, *Leading Creative Teams*, DOI 10.1007/978-1-4842-2056-6_9

Creativity is key. Imagine trying to get someone's attention and entice them to engage with your client's product when you're writing an out-of-home execution in seven words or less. Whether it's on a web page, a piece of collateral, or an out-of-home execution, copy is an integral part of the creative product. It is a combination of visual and verbal creativity.

Before we go any deeper, I would like to provide a blanket disclaimer: I am not a copywriter. I am a visual creative director who dabbles in copy. I have, however, worked with several great copywriters who were the inspiration for the information in this chapter. This chapter is meant as an overview of copywriting to support not only art directors, but also copywriters who want to progress to creative director. Ok, 'nuff said. Let's get started...

# Writing Framework

Copywriters don't simply jump into an assignment and start writing. They think about the framework of what they're trying to say first. Just like effective designs are built on certain underlying principles and fundamental elements, you can use some basic structures to write more effective solutions to your client's marketing challenges. Four common frameworks are

- **Star, Story, Solution.** Write a story that shares how the main character (the star) is going through some of the same issues that your target audience is going through right now. Develop the story to provide the reader with a hint of their personality or some of their traits to get them to either like or dislike the star, to relate to the character. Once you do this, you can begin to write the solution. The solution shows how the star worked through their issue using the product or service offered by your client.

- **Attention, Interest, Desire, Action.** Get the audience's attention. Once you have their attention, try to gain their interest with what you have to offer. Then you move into desire. Get them to believe they want or need your product or service. They must be able to picture themselves benefitting from the offer in some way. Finally, everything should work together so your call to action will get them to do something. Be clear with this. There should be no question about what the audience needs to do—call this number now, go online, eat more.

- **Problem. Agitate. Solution**. Start by identifying the problem that the target market has right now. Agitate the audience to intensify the consequences of this problem.

You are trying to emphasize that there is a problem they need to have solved. You've created a desire for a solution. With your solution, you are showing the reader how and why your client's product or service solves their problem.

- **Feel. Felt. Found.** Tell the customer you know how they feel. Empathize with their problem. Let them know that you felt the same way, but you found a solution to the issue and now you feel better. Invite them to take the same actions you have to solve their issue.

# Headline Frameworks

Headlines lead most copy executions that are used in print or online and give readers a hint of what's to come. They are typically typeset in a larger font size than the rest of the piece and have some kind of punch to them. Headlines are a catchy way to grab your target audience's attention. Regardless of the medium, there are four themes for headlines: self-interest, news, curiosity, and ease. All four entice the reader to invest time in the rest of the advertising copy. All four should engage in their own ways. Take a closer look:

- **Self-interest.** It's all about YOU. If the word "you" is in the headline, it's a self-interest headline. It leads the reader to want to find out something that is directed specifically at them. Leading an ad with a self-interest headline provides a hint that the body copy will answer specific questions: "What will this product do for me? Why should I care? Why do I want to purchase this?" The copy must provide the target audience with answers in a direct and understandable way.

- **News.** News headlines announce something that is so important to a reader that they will want to find out about it. The headline usually implies that the product or an aspect of it did not previously exist and the product is a solution to a long-standing problem. Headlines about a study, something done in a new way, breakthroughs, introductions, and so on all point to news headlines.

- **Curiosity.** Many times the word "secret" is used to garner curiosity from readers. This type of headline draws the audience in by posing a statement or question that invites them to think or answer a question. The headline can present a secret that holds the promise of doing something that the reader wants, while remaining open-ended enough to entice the curious reader to read the copy.

- **Ease.** This type of headline implies that the information about the product or service is so amazing that the reader will feel better for having read all it has to offer. The headline defines a complex problem that many people are dealing with, while offering a quick and easy solution.

No matter what their theme, some of the most successful headlines meet three prerequisites:

- *Headlines must catch the target's attention* by getting them to believe they need your client's product or service, they have the money to pay for it, and they are in a position to buy it now.

- *Headlines should make a promise* that your client's product or service can deliver upon.

- *Headlines should introduce the rest of the copy* so readers who were made curious by the promise made in the headline will find what they are looking for in the body copy.

When working up different headlines, remember certain words that can be used to begin your headline framework, such as "new," "now," "how to," "why," "because," "if," "presenting," "finally," "wanted."

Writing headlines is no easy task. Not only do you need to ensure that you have impact, but you've got to do it with the fewest words possible. No matter how great you are at writing headlines, there will be times when you are drawing a blank and could use some help. Worry not, true believer! The following is a list of prompts to fall back on when you just can't seem to come up with the correct wording.

In addition to specific words that can and have been used in headlines, there are also some typical fill-in-the-blank solutions that have been used in headlines such as

- How _____ makes me _____
- Are you _____ ?
- How I _____
- Secrets of _____
- How to _____
- Give me _____ and I'll _____

Please don't misunderstand: the headlines you produce for your client's should not be formulaic. They should be unique to the client, product, or service. If you can have a little fun with word play or alliteration, by all means do. While fun and funny headlines may win you awards or get you noticed, you must keep in mind that you are not producing work just so you can enter it into *Communication Arts* or *HOW*. In the following, I will review the different types of writing that most copywriters must be able to gain some expertise in.

# Writing Classification

Think of every way you communicate the benefits of your client's product, service, or organization. You write about how it will help customers. You tell stories of others who have used it. You describe the company. You relate stories that show customers you understand what they do and you want to help. You may write a script for a TV commercial or a radio spot. For every example listed, there are two or three types of copy that can be utilized.

Typically clients will come to you with an idea of what they need. They may come requesting that you write copy for a brochure or a billboard. As creative lead you should help them determine the best way to communicate with their customers. To be able to adequately service your clients, you must be able to write for various classifications. What are the classifications?

- **By product:** letter, brochure, direct mail, and so on.
- **By medium:** video, print, web, audio, and so on.
- **By style:** hard sell, scare, straight shot, and so on.

There are infinite variations on each classification, but there are some that are most typical. I'll review each briefly and describe why and when you might use them.

# Product

The products that you'll write for will take different forms. Each has its positive aspects as well as some limitations. The product that you provide to your client will be determined by the type of message and the goal of the communication.

- **Brochure.** A brochure is a great catchall for clients. Typically they will include the call to action (which can be subtle), the product information or message, a bit about the company or organization, and the company's unique selling proposition. Brochures work perfectly as leave-behinds, as well as for visuals during meetings and sales calls. Consider a brochure as part of the introduction or a piece of an ongoing conversation. Remember, a brochure is not the final handshake.

- **Direct marketing.** If brochures are a catchall, direct marketing is the opposite. Direct marketing is all about the pitch. All direct marketing is delivered to people who would be best suited to receive the messaging. When communicating through this route, you must communicate significance and deliver value, from the first word to the last. Use direct marketing copy when you try to access a whole new audience, reestablish contact with existing customers, or do a bit of both.

- **Poster.** This type of communication can come in the form of a print poster, a web graphic, or a billboard. Posters require brief text that communicates a lot of information in a relatively small space. Generally, the graphic element dominates, but the text can also double as the graphic. Use a poster to communicate your brand and reinforce a message the customers will encounter elsewhere, or to lead people elsewhere to obtain more information.

- **Script.** A script serves as the guide for nonwritten messaging. Scripts drive video and audio marketing. The call to action may be subtle or repeated 30 times (please don't ever do this). The manner in which you write depends on the audience, the topic, the product, and the execution.

# Medium

Whether you're considering online, print, or broadcast, they're all media. The medium is the vehicle by which the message travels, not the environment in which the audience receives it. The medium may or may not impact the collateral and style. I have to say that I don't often find that it does, but you may see it differently and I'll leave it at that.

# Style

Copywriting style is something that is unique to each writer and the items they are writing about, but there are certain styles that are best suited for different tactics.

- **Teaching.** Help consumers learn and then offer a call to action. Teaching can be used when the client isn't concerned about where the target audience buys their product as long as they buy it. Use this style to help your audience understand why they need the product. Point out features and then leave it to the audience to take action.

- **Humor.** Present your message in a way that makes your audience laugh. Humor can be self-deprecating; you might make fun of people who don't buy your product or present a funny version of a scare tactic. Use humor only if you know your audience appreciates laughter, and even then use it sparingly. While humor is fun, it's also very easy to offend your audience.

- **Straight shot.** Describe what you have, why yours is best, and why your client can deliver on their promise.

- **Scare tactic.** Deliver your message by warning customers what will happen if they do or do not listen to you. Make it clear that they should listen for their own safety: fasten your seat belt, don't drink and drive, don't smoke. Try scare tactics when you believe people will respond and there's more at stake than a sale.

- **Hard sell.** Buy now! Today for a limited time! Like the scare tactic, this style has a somewhat less than stellar reputation. It's a challenge to do it right without coming off as tacky, pushy, or demanding. On second thought, it's pretty tacky and pushy no matter how you treat it.

To be an effective copywriter, you should have a solid understanding of the types and styles of writing in order to determine the best way to communicate your client's messaging effectively. For example, you wouldn't use humor for a drinking and driving campaign in the same way you would not want to use graphic scare tactics for a diaper campaign. While most copywriters may have one or two styles they are most comfortable with, as creative director—regardless of whether you are an art leader or copy leader—you must be able to lead your team to provide messaging that is appropriate to your client and their messaging needs.

# Writing for Your Client's Target Market

When we begin writing assignments, part of the information we receive in the client brief deals with their target market—that massive group of people that the client wants to focus all of their communication toward. Are they speaking to Boomers? How about Moms? How we can forget Millennials or Centennials? When considering the target market, there is a problem that you and your creative team will face: who specifically are you speaking to?

What if your client wants to target their messaging toward Millennials? You know, that little group of people whose ages range from 19 to 35 in 2016 and now number 75.4 million? How do you target a group of people that is as diverse as this one? Millennials range in experience and age from recent high school gradu-ates to armed forces veterans who are married with children and everyone else in between. How can you speak to all of them? Easy solution: you don't.

Instead, dig deeper into the client's target audience. Who *specifically* in the Millennial group does the client want to speak to? Narrow your focus to spe-cific people, rather than trying to reach an imagined conglomeration of many different people. Create a psychographic for a specific person in the audience who you want to speak to. Give that person a face and a backstory. The fol-lowing is a sample psychographic for a Millennial fashionista living in New York City who is the target for an urban clothing line.

---

### Sample Fashion Psychographic

**Gwyneth—young professional**

**Age:** 25 years old

**Location:** New York, NY

**Relationship Status**: Serious boyfriend

**Living Status:** Rents an apartment with friends in Washington Heights

**Education:** Hofstra University major in journalism

**Work:** Account executive at Dentsu (international advertising agency)

**Car:** Doesn't have one. Uses public transportation.

**Finances:** Paying off student loans and living expenses, no savings

**Social Life/Activities:** Hanging out with friends, nightclubs on weekends, CrossFit, running

**Favorite Magazines:** *People*, *Vogue*, *Shape*

**Favorite Television:** *Game of Thrones*, *IT Crowd*, *House of Cards*, *Big Bang*

**Shops:** Bebe, Nordstroms, H&M

**Primary Need:** Looking for sophisticated styles at an affordable price. Her work requires a professional look, but she doesn't have to be over-the-top formal.

**Loves:** Name brands (even if they are fake), looking and feeling good, fresh fruit, sparkling water, fruity mixed drinks

**Where She Buys Shoes:** Nordstrom Rack, Saks Off Fifth, Macy's

---

Once I have a vision of a specific person that fits within the target demographic, I can work on copy and visuals that speak specifically to her. I can imagine different things about her: What does she like? What is she afraid of? What makes her angry? What makes her happy? Does she have her own slang or mannerisms? These are the different characteristics that you should know so you can effectively target your communication toward them.

## Unique Selling Proposition

A unique selling proposition (USP) is the one specific trait that a product, service, or organization can claim as their own. It's something that no one else can claim. It's what sets them apart from everyone else. Over the years, customer behavior has changed. Now that we are so connected it's not enough to simply state your USP and think it will get customers to engage with your client. Instead your client's USP must be understood and your client must be able to use it to deliver significance. A USP will appeal to just the right niche audience and should target people who—if they start to read about what your client is offering—will want to know more. To connect with customers, your client's USP must provide value in the form of a return on the time they have invested.

The target audience will pay with their time. The value delivered with the copy can affect their entire relationship with a brand. Some believe that copywriting is not a creative art. They believe it's a mechanical, formulaic discipline where anyone who writes creatively will go for a paycheck and eventually allow any creativity they have to wither and die. That couldn't be further from the truth. There are many creative copywriters out there who have mastered the way in which to reach their audience with compelling titles, great wordplay, and insightful messaging. It takes creativity to be successful as a copywriter. I love how some of my copywriting colleagues have been able to balance creativity with a real focus on a call to action. I believe that copywriting is one of the most difficult of writing disciplines.

## Call to Action

To successfully communicate a call to action, copywriting must deliver significance to those who are interested in or engaged with the product, service, or organization. It also needs to be worthy of attention to those who may never buy but will spread the word.

You and your creative team always want to motivate the reader to take some type of action—whether that action be physical or mental. In order to encourage people to act, there must be something to act upon. A call to action is typically the final line in an advertisement that asks the reader to do something specific. Whether it's to go online to visit a particular website or to call a phone number for more information, there is an action being requested.

The call to action can't be something akin to the conclusion of a book, where readers simply close it and set it aside. You want them to continue to engage.

## Final Tips

Before you send off your copy to be dropped into a design or to be approved by the client, be sure to read what you wrote aloud. When we write, things sound fantastic in our heads, but once we read them aloud we find things like typos or words that don't flow together. When you're reading aloud you will also be able to hear the rhythm of the sentences. Add some variety to your sentence length. Keep things interesting for the person who is the target of your copy.

Focus on your product's benefits in a way that it will always answer the question, "why should I care?" When you get them to care, and you touch on their heart and mind and make them feel something, you can recommend a course of action for them.

The one last recommendation I have for you is that you should write so anyone will understand what you're telling them. No $25 words. Keep it light, informative, engaging, entertaining, whatever you want, but absolutely keep your copy approachable.

## In a Nutshell

Copywriting is not for everyone. It is an art that can be mastered by people who love words. Just like most of what creatives do, the act of copywriting can be seen by some as a skill that anyone can master. That belief is one of the most frustrating things that creatives have to deal with. Everyone fancies themselves a creative. Everyone knows how to write, so of course they should be able to write copy... uh, yeah... not so much.

Great writing may seem effortless, but it's not. It delivers messaging in ways that resonate with the intended audience directly and without fluff. On the surface it may appear to be something that is obvious, but that couldn't be further from the truth. A lot of thought goes into (almost) every ad, every TV spot, every out-of-home, every website, and so on. The copy doesn't just magically come out of a copywriter's head. It takes creativity and skill.

The best copy will also be based on a solid foundation of strategy. Without strategy, everyone is simply knocking out ads based on what they personally like or what they believe. No bueno. Copywriters understand the nuances of the given target audience. Great copywriters are able to transcend the mundane and find the sweet spot in every writing assignment.

As I mentioned at the beginning of this chapter, copywriting isn't only about selling goods or services, it also works to motivate customers to take some type of action. If you have a specific outcome in mind, good copy can help achieve that outcome. Great copywriting can do that and entertain or engage.

The purpose of this chapter is not to teach you how to be a copywriter. If you are a copywriter on your way up the leadership chain, you should already know this. If you are an art director who seldom does any writing and relies on his or her copy partner to provide copy, this is a great time to learn what your partner does (if you don't already know.) Regardless, all creative leaders should know and understand the work that goes into copywriting so they can lead their teams when the time comes.

# CHAPTER 10

# The Art of TV and Radio

## Here's the beef

When considering this chapter, I wondered if I was getting a little too tactical. I am providing one view into what it takes to knock out a TV or radio spot, but that's not really what this book is about. As a whole, my rationale for creating this book was to help creative directors and other creative leads prepare for leadership. If I were to consider writing chapters for every element that lies within the realm of a creative lead I would have chapters on design software, illustration, poster design, editorial design… and much more than could fit into one book.

So, why did I get tactical with a 30-second TV or radio spot and dedicate a chapter to them? Because producing elements for broadcast is one of the skills that creative directors must excel at, but it's not something typically taught to them in school. Students that are going through design school or a creative sequence are required to take courses in art direction, typography, interactive media, digital illustration, or animation. Students interested in becoming copywriters will take courses in marketing, creativity, American culture, the psychology of advertising, or design of integrated communications. Whether studying to be a visual or verbal creative, students are offered classes concentrating on the skills for their particular focus, but working on TV spots or radio spots isn't part of their curriculum.

© Eleazar Hernández 2017
E. Hernández, *Leading Creative Teams*, DOI 10.1007/978-1-4842-2056-6_10

# The Bottom Line

Yes, I know. People usually put the bottom line at the end of their process, but I'm adding it here. Here's the bottom line about working on TV or radio spots: You and your team are going to work your asses off during every stage of the process, from the initial client brief through post-production. You have to pay attention to every single detail at all times. Every decision you make needs your full attention because a shoot can go awry very quickly. When you've finished shooting, unless you have a client with an unlimited budget, there is no going back to reshoot. Keep your eyes open. Make your decisions count. When you think you've done everything you can, double- and triple-check everything. If you let up at any time, there is a risk the spot will suffer. It's exhausting but when you have a great spot all the hard work is worth it.

# The Creative Brief

Every great journey begins with a story, and for the 30-second spot, that story lives in the creative brief. A creative brief is a document that is produced as a result of initial meetings and discussions between a client and the agency before any work begins. A good creative brief answers several questions: What is this project? Who is project speaking to? Why are we engaging in this project? Where and how will it be used? Throughout the creation of the project, the creative brief always provides the guidelines for the work.

Creative directors along with Account Service will be involved in composing the brief. A good creative leader can tell when there is fertile ground in a strategy. There will be nuggets of information that will get you thinking about different possibilities for creative solutions. As you come up with these key insights, when you add them to the brief, they will in turn, get your creative team energized and actively ideating solutions.

Yes, creative briefs may be tedious to work on, but it will make the entire creative process a whole lot easier in the end. For smaller jobs for clients with whom you have a long history, it may not be necessary to have a creative brief. You may know their brand standards, their voice, the visuals they utilize, and so on, and you can lead your team with a simple work order from Account Service. However, when beginning a large job or working on a TV spot, a creative brief is imperative, because it helps ground your team and gives them parameters to strive for.

Here are a few reasons that you'll want to ensure that there is a creative brief produced:

- It gets your client and creative team in alignment. It allows the client to understand the creative aspects that will be addressed and your creative team to understand what the client's goals and parameters are for the project.

- It helps make the creative process run a little faster because it will clear up any potential misunderstandings before the project commences.

- It places responsibility on specific people because it clearly outlines every aspect of the project and who is responsible for each portion of it. This guarantees accountability.

- A brief can minimize the approval process because the creative that is produced for client sign-off will be aligned with the previously approved brief.

- It guarantees a better outcome because preplanning and aligning to the brief allow the entire team to avoid unnecessary risks and problems that could take their focus away from the most important aspects of the gig.

When you receive a creative brief to get the work started, it should be relatively short. You don't want to provide too much information because it can be overwhelming. You want to have enough room for your creative team to play. When you're working with your planner or your account team to develop the creative brief, you should strive to keep it very targeted and succinct. If you can keep the brief to one page, you will have an easier time getting to the meat of the assignment. The brief should get to the key insight. What is it about the client, product, or service that the brief is really trying to get across to the public? The more specific the problem to be solved, the better. For example, instead of a brief that revolves around the idea "beer is good," provide a brief that revolves around the idea "beer is good because it doesn't fill you up."

The brief should provide the following information about the client and the assignment:

- **Key Fact:** What is the key insight about the client, product, or service that the creative team can build their ideas on?

- **Problem:** What is the problem that the campaign will solve? (e.g., too many people are texting while they are driving)

- **Objective:** What is the campaign trying to accomplish? (e.g., decrease the number of people who text while driving)

- **Key Benefit, Promise, or Offer:** What is the benefit that the target audience will experience because of the campaign? (e.g., decreasing the amount of texting on the roads can lead to fewer traffic accidents due to distracted driving)

- **Support Information:** Are there any stats that support the problem?

- **Tone:** What is the overall feeling of the campaign? (i.e., happy, sad, serious, informative, upbeat, etc.)

- **Target:** Who is the campaign speaking to?

- **Competition:** What are the client's competitors doing in the market?

- **Mandatories:** What must be done/shown? (i.e., logo, tagline, music, graphics, etc.)

Whatever you do, don't let your excitement for getting a new project allow you to run amok and start ideating before a creative brief has been created. Take it one step at a time. Wait for the brief so you have a path to follow. In the end, doing so will save you a lot of time, frustration, and money.

*One last insight:* Agency production should be involved once you begin solidify-ing the concepts. Production is an integral part of the creative department. If they are there when you have the smallest spark of an idea beginning to form, they can start thinking about how to get it accomplished.

# The Creative Process

Complete immersion in the product is a must if you and your team are going to ideate and produce work that is true to the brand and relevant to the consumer. To help your team get immersed in the project you will need to help them with research. If you don't have a planning department to provide you with research, you will need to do your own and disseminate it to your creative team. Some creative leads begin with an intuitive search online. They begin with the client and then start fishing around with a keyword search to generate a pool of visuals that can inspire their creative solutions.

To get started, I typically spend quite a bit of time writing down everything I know about the client, their target audience, and their marketing objective. This is not an exercise to begin with ideation. It's simply a way to get all of the information I know about the client out in the open. Once I put everything down on paper, I leave it behind for a while. While I am off doing other things, I allow myself to process the information and ideas start rising to the surface.

Next, I like to get a little more concrete with my ideas and start to write them out so they aren't merely abstract thoughts and visuals roaming around in my head without any real purpose. When I have my initial thoughts in a somewhat comprehensible format, I engage one of my creative team members. I typically choose a person who is suited for the marketing challenge, whether that be a design challenge, a communications challenge, a web challenge, or a broadcast challenge. If you want more about this part of the creative process, check out Chapter 5.

As you're working through the process, you'll likely find that a lot of ideas pop up in the beginning. Most of these you should throw out. If they are the first ideas that come to mind, chances are they are not very insightful and could have been thought up by anyone. Keep working at it, and eventually you will have a breakthrough. Ideas will flow from you like someone just opened a fire hydrant in the neighborhood.

# Storyboards

Storyboards are visual references used in the creation of a TV spot (Figure 10-1). They are used throughout the ideation, development, and production process. The storyboard will first be used as a visual piece presented to your client for approval. Once past that stage, it will be used by your production company to help them create their visual treatments for agency approval. Finally, once filming begins, the storyboard acts as a roadmap of the initial concept that must be used to ensure that the overall message and initial concept are not lost in the translation from static boards to completed spots.

**HERNÁNDEZ DESIGN COMPANY**

| | |
|---|---|
| Title: | Cowboys Fanatics |
| Language: | English |
| Length: | 30 Sec |
| Client: | ArchPoint/Dallas Cowboys |

**VIDEO**

Open on a neighborhood. In slow motion we see a group of men and women gathered around the back of a truck.

The truck is decked out with Dallas Cowboys decorations. Stickers, window clings, and a flag.

People, all decked out in Cowboys clothing and hats, are laughing and roaring getting psyched up for a game. In the center of the crowd we notice a man with face/body paint cooking.

Behind him we see bags of hardwood and mesquite brickettes and Fire Starter.

People are grabbing spicy and original barbecue sauces to pour on their burgers as they eat. Some are opening cutlery as they prepare to eat potato salad.

Others are finished and are wiping their hands and face with Tackle Towels and cutlery.

Mom bends down and wipes off a painted child's face with Kleenhanz towelettes. Show a quick shot of the entire family.

Logo: Dallas Cowboys
Graphics: Shot of products
Super: Find Dallas Cowboys branded products at your favorite Texas grocery store.

**AUDIO**

SFX: Hard driving music (similar to NFL highlights)

MVO: The Johnson family: Dallas Cowboys fans as long as they can remember.

MVO: Their pre-game festivities include Dallas Cowboys products: Mesquite hardwood and charcoal briquets, Fire Starter, spicy and original barbeque sauce, and cutlery packs.

MVO: For clean-up they use Tackle Towels...

MVO: and Kleenhanz towelettes.

MVO: Johnson family you're a body paint wearin', tailgate partyin', Cowboys group with supplies to match and the Dallas Cowboys love you.

Find Dallas Cowboys branded products at your favorite Texas grocery store.

**Figure 10-1.** Storyboard for a 30-second TV spot

Because storyboards provide the template or bible for the shoot, they must be clear and easily understood by everyone involved in the production. Shorthand or jargon only understood by you and your team has no place on the storyboard. Always create storyboards that can relay the key information of the concept without you having to explaining them.

In addition to universally understood storyboards, you must also be able to speak the lingo. You should understand shot list terminology to be able to describe the specific camera movements and angles that can add to the effectiveness of your spot.

# Shot List Terminology

When you're working on a storyboard to give to your production company, you can add terminology that will explain exactly what you're thinking using few words. Familiarity with the language of filmmaking is key to creating concise descriptions of each shot and avoiding the miscommunication or faulty assumptions that can be costly in terms of time and money. The following is a list of useful terms and definitions that are organized into categories of scale, angle, movement, and transition. Keep in mind that these shot terms are for your reference and should *never* be used when pitching an idea to a client. For more on this, refer to Chapter 8.

## Scale

- **Extreme close-up (ECU):** A shot with a very narrow field of view that gives the impression that the camera is very close (Figure 10-2). For example, a shot of a person's eyes.

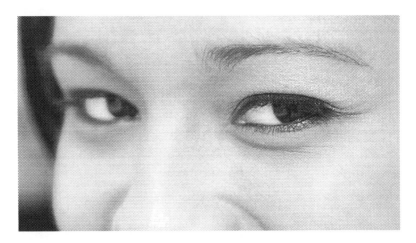

**Figure 10-2.** Extreme close-up (ECU)

- **Close-up (CU):** Same as ECU, but with a slightly larger field of view. For example, a shot of a person's head and shoulders.

- **Medium shot (MS):** A shot where the field of view is between the long shot and the close-up (big surprise, I know). The actor is typically viewed from the waist up.

- **American / Hollywood / cowboy or knee shot:** A shot that frames the talent from the knees up.

- **Full figure:** Shot composed with the entire human figure in frame (Figure 10-3).

**Figure 10-3.** Full figure

- **Long shot (LS):** A shot giving a broad view of the visual field. The subject appears to be far away from the camera.

- **Wide shot (WS):** A shot that shows a wide vista. (i.e., a horizon)

- **Single:** A shot with only one person.

- **Two shot:** A shot with two people in it.

- **Insert:** Often shot by a second camera, this shot typically reveals details either not seen in the master shot or missed by general coverage. (e.g., a hand pulling money out of a wallet)

- **Two-T shot:** A shot framed from the nipples up. (Call me immature, but this definition always makes me giggle.)

## Angle

- **High angle:** A shot taken from an angle above the object.

- **Aerial shot:** A very high angle shot, now typically accomplished with a drone.

- **Low angle:** A shot taken from an angle that places the camera below the object or subject (Figure 10-4).

**Figure 10-4.** Low angle

- **High Hat shot:** An extremely low angle shot positioned as if the camera were sitting on top of a tall hat on the ground. This view is named after a piece of equipment that is designed to hold the camera on the floor.

- **Profile:** Shot from a side angle.

- **Straight on or frontal:** When the camera angle is directly facing the subject or object.

- **3/4 shot:** A shot positioned halfway between a directly frontal angle and a profile that can be taken from the front or behind.

- **Over-the-shoulder shot (OTS):** A shot taken from over a character's shoulder, many times used during a conversation with another character.

## Camera Moves

- **Dolly shot:** Also known as a *Tracking* or *Trucking* shot. The camera rolls on dolly tracks. Usually used to record shots moving on the z axis (pushing in or pulling out).

- **Pan:** The camera swivels on the horizontal x axis, often to follow the action.

- **Swish pan:** A very swift pan that blurs the scene in between the starting and ending points.

- **Tracking shot:** Camera moves to the left or right. Typically used to follow a figure or vehicle.

- **Tilt:** The camera pivots up and down from its base.

- **Boom shot:** The camera travels up and down on a boom arm.

- **Crane shot:** A shot taken from a crane that has the ability to boom down and track in long distances without using tracks.

- **Car mount:** A shot taken from an apparatus that is mounted to a car.

- **Static shot:** Any shot where the camera does not move.

- **Steadicam shot:** A shot using the Steadicam, a camera that attaches to a harness and can be operated by a single person in handheld situations. The shots taken appear to have been done with the smoothness of a tracking shot.

- **Zoom:** The movement of a zoom lens to bring the subject closer (Figure 10-5).

**Figure 10-5.** Zoom

- **Zolly:** A technique in which the camera dollies in and zooms out at the same time, or the reverse (zooms in and dollies out simultaneously).

- **Smash zoom:** A very fast zoom.

- **Handheld:** The operator braces the camera on the shoulder or at hip height.

- **Follow shot:** Any moving shot that follows the actor.

- **Traveling shot:** Any shot that utilizes a moving camera body.

## Editing, Transitions, and Camera Point of View

- **Objective shot:** The camera sees the scene from an angle not seen by a character in the scene.

- **Subjective shot:** A shot taken from the position of someone in the scene. A Point of View (POV) shot is an example of a subjective shot.

- **Master shot:** Also known as a *Cover* shot. Typically a medium- to wide-angle shot of a scene that runs for the duration of the action.

- **Establishing shot:** Many times this is a wide shot of the location used to tell the audience where they are (Figure 10-6).

**Figure 10-6.** Establishing shot

- **Coverage:** All the setups needed to edit the scene.

- **Offscreen (OS):** Describes what is heard but not seen on the screen.

- **Reaction shot:** Usually a close-up of a character reacting silently to actions they have just seen or dialogue they are hearing.

- **Cutaway:** An editing term used to define information not seen in the master or previous shot.

- **Jump cut:** An editing term for successive shots that can cut in on the same axis. It can also be used to describe successive cuts that disrupt the flow of time or space.

- **Match cut or Match Dissolve:** Cutting or dissolving from one similar composition to another.

- **Point of View (POV) shot:** The camera angle takes the view of a character in the scene.

- **Reverse angle:** A shot that is 180 degrees opposite the preceding shot.

# Budgets

When you're working with your team to ideate TV spots, nobody ever wants to have budget constraints hamper the creative process. The reality, however, is that you have to continually aware of how much money your client has to spend and how best to allocate that money to get the job done. You should work closely with your account team to see if they have received a budget amount from the client to help you gauge whether the ideas you'd like to move forward with are feasible or not.

To develop your budget, you'll need to know what it's going to cost to produce the commercial and what it'll cost to air after it's completed. The cost to produce and air a TV spot will vary depending on several factors such as the following:

- How elaborate do the spots need to be? How much will talent cost?

- Will it be a timed buy or a complete buyout of rights?

- Are you buying local, regional, or national rights?

- Where will the spot be aired?

- Is the spot simple or complex?

- Will it require multiple setups?

- Where will it be filmed?

- How long will the spot be: 15 seconds, 30 seconds, or 60 seconds?

Budgets present an interesting dilemma. Do you find out what your budget is before speaking to production companies to get bids, or do you speak to production companies to get bids and then go to your client with the numbers and get approval? It can go either way. The "correct" approach is all based on your clients. Either way you go, prices vary, but a general rule is, "The more intricate the concept is and the faster the turnaround time, the higher the price will be."

# Production Company

Finding a good production company is critical to getting a great spot produced. You will find that there are production companies that offer the entire package of video and audio while others only offer video, which means you will have to also team with an audio studio for sound design. As you gain experience with TV spots you will work with several different companies and find that some are better than others for certain types of spots. Some can do 3D work, while others are better with live talent. Some work quickly and keep the crew small, while others are better suited for larger productions. You will get to know the people who do the best work for you.

If you're a creative lead who is just getting your first TV gig going, however, you will need to do some research. My first recommendation is calling other creative leads to obtain recommendations on production companies. As you have moved up in the ranks, hopefully you have developed friendships with others in our industry who will be willing to help you. Give them a call and ask for their advice on production companies they've used in the past.

Once you do that, call the recommended company and interview them. Have a long list of questions prepared and specifically ask to see work that was already produced for TV. Ask if they have experience in filming the specific kind of spot you are producing or if they have experience with your type of client. This will help you get an idea of what you can expect from the company when they work for you. Be sure to ask for a "demo reel" that shows snippets of multiple commercials the company has created so you can get an idea of the level of quality the firm produces on multiple projects.

Once you make it past the phone calls and narrow your candidates down to two or three, you should meet with the production companies in person. When meeting with the production company, have an idea of what you want to see, or a "vision" of what the commercial should present to your target audience. The company that's producing your commercial should be able to translate your vision into reality.

Do your homework and don't be afraid to ask as many questions as you need to. Request a contract that outlines the scope of the project along with the start and delivery dates and milestones to expect during the actual production. Clarify exactly what you're being charged for and why.

Once you assign the job, you can expect that you will receive a director's treatment. The director will create a document that outlines how he plans to turn your ideas into reality. Be open to directors' suggestions, because they are experts in bringing spots to life; just make sure they don't lose sight of your original concept and vision. As you work through the process, you will meet the members of the team who will be producing your commercial. Most good production companies will assign you a project manager to act as a liaison between you and the production team.

# Sound Design

Whether you are recording voice on camera (VOC) or you are planning to have a voice-over (VO) recorded separately, you will need to have some sound design worked up. As mentioned previously, you can either work with a production company who can handle this portion of the production or contract with a dedicated audio production company.

For the sake of argument, let's say that you need to get another production partner involved. Typically, you will either receive a recommendation from your video production company or already have someone in mind because you may have worked with them in the past and enjoyed the experience.

If you partner with the right sound company, they will work hard to ensure that you have very little to worry about when it comes to the production. It is crucial that the sounds, voice, and music work harmoniously in the spot and don't fight each other for attention. Sound design balances ambient sounds, sound effects, music, and voice to support the visuals and produce a spot that promotes your client and their product or service well.

As creative lead, you must have a good ear for all of the elements that will be added or adjusted in the spot. Work closely with your video and audio production companies. If things aren't feeling right, say so. If you think some of the sounds need to be bumped up or pulled back, let them know. Be sure of yourself. Be decisive and share your opinions. The worst thing you can do is not say anything. Time is money and the more time your video and audio partners have to spend going back and forth making edits and tweaks, the more likely it is that they will go over budget and will need to adjust what they are providing or ask for more money.

# The Radio Spot

Radio advertising—whether on traditional broadcast radio, Pandora, Spotify, iTunes Radio, or any other location where the medium of choice is sound rather than video—is a powerful way of reaching your target consumers. Radio spots vary in time from 15 to 30 to 60 seconds or even more. Although 30 seconds might not seem like much time, historically agencies have utilized this time block to transmit messages quite successfully. There are a few things that are relatively obvious, but they must be part of your spot to make it as effective as possible.

## Mention the Product

The client, product, or service should be introduced at the top half of the spot. Some believe that it should be mentioned immediately at the beginning of the spot. Ideally, the mention should also be combined with creating or identifying a need. For example, if you are trying to get people to purchase pizza, your 30-second spot could start with, "Need dinner fast? Broadway Joe's has just what you're hungry for." With this strategy, you have managed to introduce the need and the product within the first 10 seconds of the spot. The beginning of the ad always should grab the listener's attention by offering to solve a problem. This helps the listener pay attention to the rest of the message.

## Discuss Its Benefits

Now that you've grabbed the listener's attention, quickly discuss the benefits that your client's product has to offer. Focus on the main benefit or offer and keep it short. You don't want to rush through the spot and confuse the audience. You could say, "Broadway Joe's has been proven as a pizza leader for over 10 years. We only use the freshest ingredients to ensure that your meal will taste great."

## Offer an Enticement

After sharing why the product is great, you must offer a reason for listeners to care and entice them to act. This can be in the form of a special offer that is only available to people who hear the 30-second spot and use a code that you will provide. For example, "You can get a medium two-topping pizza for just $5.99 if you use our listener-only special code. Give us code: JoeKnowsPizza, and you're as good as gold." Entice the listening audience with a strong incentive and remind them that only they qualify for this special deal.

# The Call To Action And Reminder

Finally, you need to close the ad with a quick call to action and reminder about the product. For example, "Call us or visit us online to place your order and get your two-topping pizza for just $5.99. We've got the best pizza in town! Broadway Joe's!" By giving listeners multiple ways to contact the client and take part of the offer, you increase the chance of success. In addition, by having customers use a code that was only offered via radio, you have a great way to track the successfulness of the spot. Win-win.

# Producing The Radio Spot

A well-produced radio spot can inspire the imagination and get people thinking about your client's service or product. Without a video, the listener's mind is free to wander. They have every opportunity to imagine any type of scenario that you provide as long as you can grab their attention, hold their interest, get them to laugh, or most importantly, get them to pay attention. You must keep in mind that people who are listening to the radio are typically doing something else at the same time whether that's driving to work or school, sitting at the office or at home, or exercising in a gym. So, go into it knowing that they might not listen to every word. This forces you to ensure that every word they hear is succinct and impactful!

When you create your spot, you want to use a standardized format. Standardizing is very important, because you want people to know they are hearing a commercial for the same businesses even if they hear slightly altered versions.

To standardize the sound of the spots you can

- Request to use a female or male voice on all spots.

- Request the same music.

- Spell out the kind of energy you want put into the voice ("energetic read" or "laid-back, casual read").

- Create spots with the same type of format (problem/ solution, narrative, character driven).

You can familiarize people with your spots by the way you execute them. Consistency breeds familiarity. Familiarity can breed loyalty and sales—that's what we want.

Once you've knocked out the basics and received client approval on your scripts it's time to get in the studio. You will need to reach out to several sound studios to get pricing. Once you determine who you're going with, you will need to provide them with the specifications of what type of voice and read you want. Once you've selected the talent and received client approval on the

voice, it's time to go. Get in studio and work with the editor and talent to produce the spot you want. Get a full range of different takes—different energy
levels, different emphasis on various words, and so on. While you're in studio
recording the talent, be sure to get as many takes as possible. Once the talent
is gone, they are gone. Getting them back into the studio will cost you money.

After you've released the talent, you will work with the editor to get the spots
you've ideated. Then it's off to the client for approval. In a perfect world, you won't
receive many edits from this point and you can have the spots trafficked out.

# In A Nutshell

This chapter has been a very cursory overview of TV and radio production.
There is much more that goes into it, but this at least gives you a snippet of
information that can bolster what you know or what you may feel you were
lacking. TV production can be very enjoyable and rewarding, but it can also be
extremely exhausting and, in some cases, frustrating. What you get out of it is
completely based on what you put into it and who you partner with to produce
the work. I have had the good fortune to work with great TV production companies (Matchframe/1080, Maverick Video Productions, Sprocket Productions,
13th Floor Studios, and Cevallos Brothers Productions) and radio/sound studios
(The Living Room and Harter Music). When you have the right partners, and
hopefully a realistic budget to work with, you can accomplish great things.

It is imperative that you ensure that your client has a budget to produce a
TV or radio spot. There is nothing worse than having a client who wants TV,
but doesn't have the money to put into it. In my own experience, I have had
some great production companies reduce their prices just to get the job and
the chance at future work. The problem with doing that is twofold. First, the
client is still expecting a polished, well-executed TV spot that looks good and
sounds good on a shoestring budget. Second, it sets a bad precedent with the
client, who now gains an unrealistic expectation that any future TV spots will
cost about the same.

Your account team must provide clients with realistic estimates and be willing to have difficult conversations regarding budgets. If the client wants TV
or radio but can't afford it, then try to find another way to address their
marketing challenge. Maybe it's not a TV spot. Don't sacrifice your reputation,
the reputation of your agency, or that of your production partner by allowing
budgets to get so low that nobody is being profitable and you risk producing
work that is inferior or doesn't have a positive effect on your client's business.

That said, regardless of your budget you have a job to do. Get creative and
resourceful. Try to find ways to work inside of an approved budget and the
timeframe provided. Be honest with the team if something can't get done.
Lead your creative team and knock out some great award-winning spots that
you, your creative team, your agency, and your client will be proud of.

# Career Trajectories to Creative Leadership

## How do I get there?

Is there a magic formula or an actual outlined path that someone should follow to become a creative leader? I'd like to say in my best Yoda voice, "Path to creative leadership, yes there is." Unfortunately, almost every creative director has taken a path all his or her own. What works for one may not work for another. Senior Art Director A might be thrust into a leadership role because they happen to be in the right place at the right time. Multimedia Designer B is given responsibility and is suddenly thrust into the role of creative director as part of their in-house team, but doesn't understand the role. Newly promoted Creative Director C took the slow and steady path to creative director starting as a junior art director and, through creative blood, sweat, and tears at

© Eleazar Hernández 2017
E. Hernández, *Leading Creative Teams*, DOI 10.1007/978-1-4842-2056-6_11

the same agency, makes their way to creative leadership. More often, creative leaders grow, learn, and progress by spending time at an agency, developing expertise in their current position, and then moving on to another agency for a higher title with more responsibility.

Each path is unique, just as each creative is unique. As I review sites like LinkedIn or simply do an intuitive search online for terms like "creative director," among the creative directors at agencies and studios who have worked to earn the title, what I see are very young creatives who are freelancers, students, and so on claiming the title of creative director without the credentials. It's a problem that proliferates throughout the creative landscape.

I have been asked if there is a specific path that someone who is interested in a creative career can follow that will eventually lead them to the position of creative director. The answer is always, "Yes." But first, you must ask yourself a few questions...

# What Exactly Is a Creative Director, and Do I Really Want to Become One?

Creative directors lead teams of creatives who are responsible for conceptualizing, developing, and producing work that addresses a client's communications challenges. You will find creative directors in many different fields from advertising and design to fashion and broadcast. In terms of advertising and graphic design, most of the work that a creative director is responsible for creating comes in the form of TV spots, out-of-home advertising, advertising and branding campaigns, websites, brochures, package design, logos, and other collateral materials. Many times the creative director is tasked with managing an interdisciplinary team which includes graphic and web designers, copywriters, web designers and developers, and social media content developers. A creative director does not have to know everything about how a creative project is developed; however, they must know how to motivate and lead a team of creative professionals that does. In any given day a creative director's input may be solicited on any number and types of assignments from an advertising campaign to a brand refresh, a website design to an out-of-home execution, a TV shoot to a radio recording session, a brainstorm session to new business pitch. Knowledge and versatility are key to being a good creative director. You must be able to quickly assess the assignment given to your team, brainstorm and work with them to find the creative "sweet spot," motivate them to develop visuals and messaging that stands out in a crowded marketplace, gain approval and support from your agency team, present to a client and sell them on the idea, and be ready to start all over again.

Creative directors are considered upper-level management and as a result work under a great deal of pressure and strict deadlines. They must deal with personnel, budgets, and profitability as well as ensure that all creative products that leave the agency represent in a good light and meet deadlines, while also addressing client challenges. That said, one of the benefits of being a creative director is it usually comes with a good salary along with a good deal of creative control over the output of your team.

Here is my take on a creative direction career trajectory. Like all careers, you'll start at the bottom, and through drive and determination, can climb up the ladder. Let's take a look at a typical career progression:

## Junior Art Director / Designer / Copywriter—Entry-level

*Degree Level*: Associate's degree, bachelor's degree.

*Design Major*: Advertising, Branding, Communication Design, Graphic Design.

*Copy Major*: Journalism, Advertising, Communications, Creative Writing, Professional Writing.

*Experience*: College degree and/or previous work experience.

*Key Skills*: Must be visual thinkers who have a strong desire to work through a creative process in a team environment to produce work for clients. They must have the ability to execute designs and production files: the role is entry-level, very "hands-on," and often extremely busy.

## Art Director / Designer / Copywriter

*Degree Level*: Associate's degree, bachelor's degree, or in rare cases previous work experience.

*Design Major*: Advertising, Branding, Communication Design, Graphic Design.

*Copy Major*: Journalism, Advertising, Communications, Creative Writing, Professional Writing.

*Experience*: 2–4 years; agency, studio, or in-house experience.

*Key Skills*: Must be good at listening to instructions, contributing to brainstorm sessions, working as part of a team, understanding how to solve visual or writing problems and executing instructions. Must have a desire to work with creative teammates to understand and address clients' needs and desires. Should be familiar with a variety of elements for projects such as papers, fonts, colors, photos, and so on. Often produces work that is conceptualized by the senior-level team members.

## Senior Art Director / Designer / Copywriter

*Degree Level*: Associate's degree, bachelor's degree, or in rare cases previous work experience.

*Design Major*: Advertising, Branding, Communication Design, Graphic Design.

*Copy Major*: Journalism, Advertising, Communications, Creative Writing, Professional Writing.

*Experience*: 5–10 years; agency, studio, or in-house experience.

*Key Skills*: Must have the ability to confidently consult with clients during projects' initialization, revision, and support stages. Must have the ability to create designs and production files. Must seek out opportunities to gain managerial experience. Must be able to develop the conceptual and visual development of designs. Must be able to guide and mentor junior creative team members to execute deliverables. Must have the ability and expertise to work with vendors such as photographers, print houses, typographers, and other professionals associated with the industry as support partners.

## Associate Creative Director

*Degree Level*: Associate's degree, bachelor's degree, or in rare cases previous work experience.

*Design Major*: Advertising, Branding, Communication Design, Graphic Design.

*Copy Major*: Journalism, Advertising, Communications, Creative Writing, Professional Writing.

*Experience*: 6–10 years; agency, studio, or in-house experience.

*Key Skills*: The ability to lead a team is key. Must have intermediate interpersonal and managerial expertise. Must be able to listen to and speak with staff and clients to ensure that the employees' creative ideas and clients' desires for different assignments are in alignment. Must be skilled at conceptualizing interesting and innovative ideas and developing those ideas into marketing solutions. Must be able to explain those ideas and rationale to staff, agency teammates, and clients.

## Creative Director

*Degree Level*: Associate's degree, bachelor's degree, or in rare cases previous work experience.

*Design Major*: Advertising, Branding, Communication Design, Graphic Design.

*Copy Major*: Journalism, Advertising, Communications, Creative Writing, Professional Writing.

*Experience*: 8–12 years of experience.

*Key Skills*: Must have advanced interpersonal and managerial expertise. Must be versed in coordinating with various agency departments to assist with the successful ideation, development, and production of all assignments. Must have expertise in ideation, development, and management of creative ideas while leading multiple projects through their various stages with the creative team. Must be able to manage departmental budgets. Must be able to sell ideas to clients and maintain beneficial and profitable relationships with them.

# Do I Need a Bachelor's Degree?

While there are a few rare individuals who are able to enter the industry and are somewhat successful without the benefit of a bachelor's degree, the majority of creatives that make it to creative director hold some type of degree, in some cases, an advanced degree such as a Master of Arts or Master of Fine Arts. Beyond the benefit of enrolling in classes that will help you hone your creative skills, included in any degree plan are general education requirements that help develop creatives into well-rounded thinkers, not just do-ers.

Spending time in courses beyond the obvious art or writing classes provides creative directors with a deeper well from which to pull their thoughts when it's time to brainstorm. Information for a brand may be pulled from something learned in a history class. Inspiration might come in the form of a memory from math class. Wherever the insight comes from, a well-rounded student can arrive at solutions that are well thought out and go to a deeper level. Creative directors must use their knowledge and experience to lead their teams to develop consistent brand vocabulary for their clients. From matching fonts and colors to developing brand appeal, a well-rounded education informs a creative director's ideas and inspiration.

In terms of jobs, most employers prefer to hire creative directors with knowledge of marketing techniques as well as knowledge of art and graphic design. A bachelor's degree in design, advertising, or writing can serve as a foundation for a creative director depending on whether their specialty is visual or verbal.

If you're reading this book and you are still in school, these tips are for you:

- **Take courses outside of your major to broaden your thinking process**. Every creative in the industry who attended college will take the mandatory creative classes. What separates creatives once it's time to get a job will be not only be what's in portfolio, but how intelligent your work is and whether you can intelligently explain the rationale behind it. While the pretty picture will get someone's attention, the intelligence behind the work and the manner in which you speak about it will get you the job.

- **Experiment while you are in school**. Everyone will be trying to create work that looks like the stuff they see in *Communication Arts*, *HOW*, *Print*, or *Archive*. Honestly, that's boring. Stand out by having your own voice. You'll have your entire career to create work within client constraints. Use your college years as an opportunity to experiment with mediums, viewpoints, visuals. You have no budgets to stick to. You have no clients telling you to "make the logo bigger." You also have much more time to develop your work than what you'll have in the real world. Make a statement before you are confined to client's approvals. Push the boundaries of creativity while you can. Experiment. Have fun!

- **Take a public speaking class**. I strongly suggest that you take a public speaking class because all creatives, especially creative directors, will be required to give presentations at some point in their careers. Your presentation skills can make the difference between your agency winning or losing a pitch. You'll also need practice to remove those dreaded verbal pauses. It drives me crazy when a person's presentation is filled with more verbal pauses than actual content. Oops… I digress.

Whether you're a student or a seasoned creative looking to go to another job:

- **Create a stellar online portfolio**. Make sure you have an online presence because that's where everyone will look first. Get your work up and present it in the best way possible. Your work should load quickly whether someone is looking at it on their computer or their phone. Unless you're trying to get a job working in broadcast developing TV intros, don't worry about cutesy transitions or flashy intros. They are distracting and will annoy anyone who visits your page more than once. Keep it simple. Keep it clean.

- **Have a leave-behind portfolio.** When you head to your first interview, be sure to leave a printed and bound sampling of your work (or school work) that your potential supervisor can pass around to others who will need to provide input on your employment. I recommend a clear acetate cover with a black back and a coil spine (you can get this at FedEx Office). Don't go the staple, paper clip, or binder clip route. Your leave-behind portfolio will speak for you when you are not around. Make it sing your praises.

## Is Experience Required?

Employers typically prefer applicants with some experience. Not many employers—whether agency, studio, or in-house department—want to pay to train creatives. While in school take advantage of any internship opportunity you can.

Most internships are not paid, but sometimes you'll luck out and find one that is. Either way, get your name out there and build a reputation as a hard-working, intelligent, creative person. If you're lucky, there will be a position at one of the places where you interned. If you busted your ass while you were there, you will have a leg up on the competition. At the very least, you will have people who will be willing to write great recommendations for you when you need them.

Once you've made it to the senior art director level, take every opportunity given to you to manage someone else. Ask your creative leader for supervisory opportunities. Whether it's implementing a training program to mentor junior-level creatives, leading random or scheduled brainstorm sessions, or supervising freelancers, do it. You need to gain experience leading others in order to progress up the career ladder.

When you start interviewing for creative director positions, I guarantee the people interviewing you will ask about your supervisory experience. You'd better have an answer if you want the gig. There won't be opportunities for you to learn how to supervise people once you are hired as a creative director. Even rudimentary supervisory experience is something you should have gotten before you interviewed for your potentially new position. The people who will consider hiring a creative director will expect that you already know how to supervise. You will also need to know how to lead a team and delegate. If you are unsure of these basic requirements of being a creative director, you won't last long.

# Do I Need a Graduate Degree?

Honestly, most of the creative directors I know don't have a graduate degree. They reached the position with a bachelor's degree and lots of experience. Now don't get me wrong, an advanced degree certainly will help you along the way. When you are pursuing a master's degree you are narrowly focused on the specific degree criteria instead of having the broad overview that came during your undergraduate studies. Sometimes, creatives will find that pursuing a graduate degree in an ancillary topic would benefit them.

For example, a friend of mine at GDC Marketing + Ideation, Carey Quackenbush, one of the best creative leaders I've worked with, started his career as a copywriter. As he worked his way up the ladder he decided to pursue a Masters in Business Administration with a focus on Marketing Management. Now as Chief Ideation Officer of GDC, he utilizes what he learned while studying for his MBA along with his creative leadership skills to ensure that their client's messaging not only is creative and stands out, but also exceeds the business requirements of his client's marketing effort.

Don't get me wrong. There are plenty of creative directors or chief creative officers out there with a bachelor's degree. I am not saying that everyone needs to have a graduate degree in order to be successful. However, because of the level of study that is involved with the pursuit of a graduate degree, I believe it can help develop and broaden your level of thinking and helps you bring more to the table when it comes to ideation and leadership.

# Is Advancing to Creative Director the End of the Road?

Advancing to creative director is the culmination point for some careers, but that doesn't mean it's the end of the line. When you're in a small city or working at a small shop, the highest level you can achieve might be creative director. However, there are larger cities with larger agencies where you will find group creative directors, executive creative directors, regional and worldwide creative directors. If you're interested in reaching those heights you will need to be in a big market to do so. What are the big markets? Think New York, Los Angeles, Miami, Chicago, Dallas, San Francisco, Washington, DC.

Landing a creative gig in those large markets could prove to be a challenge if you're in a smaller market. Your chances may be very slim unless you've got something amazing to offer. New York is a particularly hard egg to crack as a creative, because there are more creatives in and around New York City than anywhere else in the world. Why would New York agencies hire someone from outside the area when there are already thousands of qualified creative people in the city, unless the creatives seeking employment had something unique to offer? ¿Me entiendes?

If you want to get into the big agencies, you need to start doing your homework now. Reach out to the agencies. See if you can find someone to connect with. Believe it or not, you may know someone who knows someone who is related to someone who works at SuperFaboo Agency. See if there is someone there with whom you can make a connection. Start a conversation. Don't get all stalker crazy, but at least reach out and find things in common.

While you're making connections, build your personal brand story. What makes you unique? What will make you a valuable addition to their company? How will you produce creative work that is different than any of the thousands of other creatives out there trying to get the same position? You must get out in front of people show them what is unique about you and your abilities. It's a jungle out there. Only those who are driven and smart will survive. You can do it, if you really want it.

# Is There an Accreditation for Creatives?

This is a question that most creatives don't even think about. Currently there is no accreditation or certification process for creatives in the United States. Several years ago as a member of the Graphic Artists Guild, I heard talk of pursuing some form of accreditation for designers, but it never went far because many creatives don't feel the need for any kind of certification system.

In Canada, however, there is a certification program for graphic designers. Graphic Design Certification (GDC) is Canada's national certification body for graphic and communication design and, since 1956, has established standards for design professionals, educators, and leaders. Through their certification program, GDC licenses the unique CGD certification mark to members whose creative services meet rigorous, standardized criteria. The CGD certification mark is recognized across Canada as the mark of professional services and ethical business conduct.

Of course, whether Canada has a certifying authority or not doesn't stop people or agencies from practicing. They claim that the accreditation allows members to say they are part of a larger organization that maintains the highest business ethics and design communications professionalism. I am not sure if something that is not governmentally mandated can have a significant impact on the design community, but they believe it can. Maybe they are right. Who am I to argue?

## Is Professional Experience Mandatory?

What role does professional experience play in the development of a creative leader? Plenty. Time and time again I have seen people who claim to be a creative director, but don't meet the criteria. I've heard things like, "My title is multimedia designer, but really I'm a creative director." Or "I started my own design studio so I decided I will be creative director."

Here are my questions/thoughts based on creative directors I have come across:

- Are you really a creative director without a creative team to direct?

- Can you really be a creative director when you just graduated from school?

- How can you be a creative director when you've never worked in an agency, a studio, or even an in-house creative department?

- Sure, when you start your own company you can give yourself any title you want. But you can't really be a creative director just because you say so.

- You can't be a creative director without any practical experience leading a group of creatives to successfully address client challenges.

Bottom line, you can call yourself a creative director if you want. You can get business cards made that say you're a creative director. You can even create a portfolio website that says you're a creative director. Be careful not to claim the position and then be commissioned for a job where they expect you to lead. It could not only cause you some embarrassment, but it could cost you money.

Real creative directors have earned that title and position through a combination of education, career, and life experience. You can gain experience by making your way through the ranks with hard work, dedication, and creativity in an agency, studio, or in-house department. It will take time… as well it should.

# Do Creative Leaders Really Need Management Skills?

Management is one of the elements that are key to the success of any creative leader. You must learn to manage people and in some cases manage budgets. How do you acquire management skills?

You can do any of the following:

- Take night courses at a local college or university.

- Enroll in online course at www.lynda.com, www.skillshare.com, or the like.

- Find a mentor and pick their brains. Honestly, this is the least successful way to do it, but it can be helpful.

- You can start small in your department with little management tasks and work your way up to larger ones.

The thing that differentiates a good leader from a great leader is the ability to drive accountability in the team. Who wants a team full of creatives who sit around and wait for the traffic manager to tell them what to do, where to go, and when to finish?

A good manager can use accountability to drive their team's performance and clarify expectations for the members of your team. You should set clear expectations for your team so they understand exactly what is expected of them and how their actions impact the entire team. I believe the key to good management is good communication.

You must be able to communicate what your expectations are to the members of your creative team as well as your agency teammates. If you can communicate them in a way that's clear you will do well. However, even with good communication skills there will be issues with personnel. Keep communicating so they know what you expect. Keep the lines of communication open. Encourage your team and work to resolve any issues that may crop up before they become major obstacles. If they are successful, give them sincere praise. Do it in private and public. Don't go over the top, but be sure to recognize them and let them know that they are appreciated.

If the unfortunate happens and someone falls short of your expectations, correct them. Do it quickly, but in a professional and respectful manner. Corrections should be done in private so you don't humiliate or embarrass anyone. Be sure to let them know what they did correctly, then let them know what needs improvement. Give them recommendations on how to correct the problem and prevent it from being a reoccurring issue. Correcting your team is sometimes difficult. It's never comfortable to have to correct someone, but it must be done. Be sure to follow up with the team member later to ensure that they are now doing what you have asked them to do in the manner in which you want it done.

If you have to correct someone more than once, it's time to put something in writing. When you write someone up be sure that you detail the cause of the letter and how they can improve. Additionally, you will need to outline possible consequences if they fail to take corrective actions. Conclude the letter with a timeframe in which they must make the correction. Be sure to follow up to check on their progress. If they correct the behavior, good. Be sure to praise the behavior. If they do not, other measures will need to be taken.

I could go into detail about management scenarios that you may encounter as a creative leader, but that might be the topic of another book. I highly recommend checking out www.lynda.com or www.skillshare.com. They have several management courses that you can watch.

# In a Nutshell

Becoming a creative director is not a golden ticket to stop learning. You will not keep your job long if you stagnate and cease growing, learning, and improving. While you don't have to understand how to do the nuts and bolts of different creative jobs, you should understand how to integrate them into a cohesive whole that solves your client's marketing challenges. The world is constantly changing. You should make every effort to stay informed about new technologies and techniques. If you don't keep abreast of things as they are developing, you will be left behind and could risk being replaced by someone that is more informed.

Whether you go back to school, take online courses, or simply read lots of books and magazines, do not let the grass grow under your feet. There are hundreds of creatives out there looking to replace you as creative leader. You can never afford to become complacent. Younger creatives don't want to hear about what you've done in the past. They don't care about the success you achieved 10 years ago. In some cases they don't care about what you did 5 years ago. They only care about the knowledge and creativity you bring to them right here right now. How can you lead them to greater heights if you are still living in the past?

You must become a student of creativity, not only of your craft, whether it's design, copywriting, web design, and so on; in addition, you must constantly learn everything. Become a sponge not only of our industry, but of the world around us. If Michelangelo (you know the guy who carved David and painted the ceiling of the Sistine Chapel) was quoted as saying, "I am still learning" when he was already at peak of his mastery, who are we to believe we can't learn more as well?

Once you've reached a position of creative leadership, do yourself a favor: don't get lazy. Keep learning. Keep pushing the boundaries of creativity. Be an early adopter of programs or apps and figure out a way of integrating them into the fabric of your creative work. Look to inspiration outside of your craft to get great ideas. Don't get too comfy with your new title. Getting comfy puts you at risk being replaced by someone who is hungrier.

CHAPTER
12

# Invest in Your People

## Here's a real ROI

One of the most frequent questions I get from other creative directors or people on their way up is, "What is the one piece of advice every good creative director should have?" My answer is simple: Invest in your people. Your team will be the ones that help you complete the day-to-day tasks and assignments that need to be knocked out to address client challenges. Your team is your go-to group when you need to get a job done after hours. Your team also has your back when people may question the direction of the creative product that your team is producing. The size of the investment you put into your people can determine the amount of success they, and in turn you, will have.

## Investment on the Front End

You need to invest in your people on the front end; whether it's from your first day leading the department or when a new team member first joins your team, don't wait until they have proven themselves. You must make the time, get the funds, or take the opportunity to invest in them as soon as you can. When you do, you are showing them that they are important and that you are making a commitment to their development. This goes a long way to gaining their loyalty.

© Eleazar Hernández 2017
E. Hernández, *Leading Creative Teams*, DOI 10.1007/978-1-4842-2056-6_12

Some creative leaders worry that putting time, money, and training into team members just makes them more attractive to other agencies or studios. Although it seems counterintuitive, you really can't worry about that. Your goal is to build the best possible team. You can't be effective if you are worrying about whether they are going to leave and take your time, money, and talent investment with them.

On the optimistic side, your investment will result in better trained, better equipped, and more motivated creative team members who appreciate the investment you have made in them and reward you with great work. On the pessimistic side, you might train someone who takes off for another company as soon as there is an opportunity. Chances are if they are that eager to leave, you may be able to see that before you make any significant investments on your part. If they take off after you have invested in them, let them go and wish them well. You can take solace in the fact that you are helping to put better creatives out in the world.

One of the things that gives me the most pride is seeing my creatives—whether they were my students or members of my team—being promoted into leadership positions and accomplishing great things.

## Invest Your Time

One of the easiest ways to invest in your people is to actually give them your time and undivided attention. As creative directors or creative leads, our time is a precious commodity. We are constantly jumping from meeting to meeting to present the agency's creative work to clients. You will be pulled into internal meetings to go over strategy and check on project progress. You will also attend staff meetings, birthday and office celebrations, and random unscheduled meetings. In addition to all of these, you will also need to try to find time to work on your own projects. In the end, it leaves little time for your people to connect with you.

There is never enough time to do everything you want or need to accomplish from day to day, and sometimes week to week. You will need to take control of your calendar and carve out some time for your team. I have reserved specific blocks of time on my calendar every day, every week so my team can have access to me. These 1-1/2 hour blocks are marked as busy on my daily calendar to prevent people from scheduling or requesting meetings when they look at my schedule. This allows me to ensure that I am present and available to my team.

Making a standing appointment that no one can schedule meetings into is a great way to reserve time for your team so you can address issues, brainstorm, provide praise, obtain updates on projects, and so on. Your team needs to feel supported and guided so they can create great work. How do you do it? The following are tips that can help you give your team the time and input they deserve.

# Roll Out

Face-to-face interactions in the office are typically the easiest ways to meet with your creative team. Sometimes, however, the best way to be inspired and to inspire others is to get the heck outta Dodge. Leave the office and find inspiration away from the office. For instance, you could

- Hold walking one-on-one meetings

- Plan team retreats involving outdoor time

- Organize a staff lunch in a local park

- Schedule ideation sessions in a botanical garden or another scenic venue

- Take your team to a museum and discuss the art you see that inspires all of you

# Be Generous, but Honest

When it comes to investing time into your team to help the department's creative output, it will be effective only if you are giving them great input, advice, or direction. When talking with your team or individual team members, be respectful, open, and honest at all times. When someone does a great job, talk about what went right and celebrate! Be generous with praise. Everyone likes and needs validation for creativity and hard work. Don't forget about the failures, however. You must address them as well. Failures can teach us quite a bit. Take the time to discuss the ideas that simply didn't work in a supportive and encouraging way with the goal of learning from them and making the next project more successful.

# Make 'Em Laugh

What kind of manager are you? Are you a stuffed shirt who seldom finds things funny? Are you laid back and approachable? While I don't advocate for trying to be the "stand-up comedian" type of boss who cracks jokes about everything, humor is an important part of a highly creative work environment (Figure 12-1). Humor can strengthen relationships, reduce stress, and make it easier to address tough subjects. Let your creative team know it's okay to goof around a little, and trust them to recognize when it's time to get down to business. Just make sure the humor is appropriate for professional interactions and isn't offensive to anyone.

**Figure 12-1.** While you don't have to be a stand-up comedian, you do need to have a sense of humor

# Invest Your Money

Investing money into your creative team can be difficult. You struggle to determine how to best invest the limited time that you have and how to effectively spread yourself among your team members to ensure they have everything they need to proceed. Do you invest small amounts into your entire team or larger amounts for a select few? It's a difficult decision to make. In a perfect world you would be able to invest resources in all of the members of your creative team, but in reality there are limits. On one hand, you want to be fair and give everyone an opportunity to increase their skills and knowledge. On the other hand, you only have so much money to go around and you want to invest it wisely. I suggest you require anyone who receives an investment of funds for training to reciprocate by sharing what they learned.

Consider the following scenario: You decide to send a designer to a national design conference that is well known for the types and caliber of breakout sessions. Many attendees return to their jobs fired up about what they learned. A good way to have your team members provide some payback for these opportunities is to have them conduct "lunch 'n learn" sessions with the rest of the team. It is their responsibility to create presentations and share what they learned with the rest of the team.

Having the team members conduct a session to share their new knowledge is a great way to receive a return on your investment because they will return with renewed enthusiasm for the job and be able to share that excitement and knowledge with their coworkers. Be sure to inform your creatives that they will be required to conduct sessions in advance. If they know there is something required of them, they are more likely to try and get as much as they can from the conference/training sessions they attend instead of viewing them as a free day out of the office or a free trip to another part of the country.

## Invest Your Expertise

Investing your expertise in your team can have a profound effect on their performance and their attitude. If you are willing to share what you know with your team, you are sending the message that you believe in them and want them to be the best possible creatives they can be. Sharing your knowledge, skills, and experience with your team can also have a positive impact for you because there is no better ROI than seeing the light bulb turn on when a new insight or skill is received and utilized by one of your team members.

How can you share your expertise? Have you ever had a junior art director attend a press check with you? Ask them to meet you at the print shop, introduce them to the press person, let them follow along as you review the press proofs and make adjustments. It is your opportunity to show them what you're looking for when you review proofs. You can explain to them how color adjustments are made on press. You can also ask your print partner to show them how they mix up spot colors. You could also ask for a tour of the print shop. This is a great chance for your team member to learn about this part of the creative process and get excited about what they do. It's also a great opportunity for you to teach them about some of the biggest mistakes designers make when it comes to print jobs and press checks.

Don't get me wrong: nobody wants to hear about the "good ol' days" of design and printing. While it may be interesting to share war stories about complex projects or all-nighters once, they don't want to continually hear about them. Share your knowledge in ways that don't sound like you're comparing what's going on now with how you did things back then. Don't brag about how your previous work or employers were superior in ways that are lacking in your current gig. Keep that crap to yourself and work on investing your expertise in positive insightful ways.

## Benefits of Investing in Your People

It's sometimes difficult to rationalize why you should invest your time, money, and expertise in your people. There is a concern that you are making your team members more marketable to other agencies or studios. That's true. There will always be people who move on to what they perceive as greener pastures (Did I just make a country reference? Pastures?! Whut?) or who follow the money tree, not realizing how good their current situation is. There will also be people who understand how fortunate they are to have a job and a creative lead who is willing to invest in them. The people described in the latter scenario are the loyal creatives who make your investments worthwhile.

The reality that you have to face is that every member of your creative team can benefit from a solid development program. The problem with team member development is that it's something that's easily pushed aside because of the pressures of meeting daily challenges. Some days you might feel it's hard enough to make it through the day without having to think about team development. However, I firmly believe that as a creative leader, you owe it to your team to make time to help them develop.

I can imagine what you're thinking: "Yeah, yeah. It's easy to talk about it. It's hard to put it into practice." Or you might think, "Sure, I agree. I'll get to it next week or as soon as we finish this RFP/TV shoot/branding campaign/etc." Don't just give it lip service, keep thinking about it, and never actually do anything. Make it a priority, or ultimately your agency or studio's product will suffer. It will suffer because your product will never evolve. You will be stuck providing the same thing over and over without any development or advancement while other agencies who evolve with changing times win the accounts you covet.

So, enough of the soapbox. Here are four reasons you should invest in your peeps.

## To Attract and Keep Great Creatives

Agencies and studios that offer a great development system to potential team members are very attractive places to people searching for new jobs or opportunities. Creatives want to work where they feel creatively challenged and are able to enhance their skills. What creative can say "no" to working in an environment when they know up front that their employer is dedicated to their advancement? Once they are onboard, employee development is a great way to help retain your team. They appreciate that you value them enough to invest in them.

How does a development program entice new creatives to join your team?

- **It's a benefit.** Current and potential employees will see the development program as an added benefit to working in your place. In the days of creatives evaluating employment options by more things than just salary as a way to determine whether they want to work somewhere, having the added benefit of professional development gives you a competitive advantage over similar jobs and salaries.

- **It creates loyalty.** Investing in your team fosters a sense of loyalty among the members, which in turn creates a sense of loyalty to the agency/studio as a whole. If your creative team feels a sense of loyalty, they are less likely to quit. If they know that you are willing to provide training and development, they will feel important and valued.

- **It builds your reputation**. No matter what you think about privacy and keeping things on the down low, people talk. If you have a reputation as a good creative leader, one who is dedicated not only to doing great work but also to ensuring that your team has opportunities for development, the word will get out. Creatives at other agencies or studios will hear about the dedication you have to your team, and you will build a rep as a great creative leader.

- **It entices good people**. Development will attract a larger pool of potential candidates to hire from when you have job openings. The development opportunities you offer to your creative team will be an added benefit that will entice good people to work with you. You want a creative who is dedicated to improving not only their craft but also themselves. Remember: you want to work with giants.

---

**Soapbox**  In regards to developing your team's skills and making them more marketable to other agencies, there are some things you should consider. People change jobs for a variety of reasons—more money, better benefits, relocating to another city, starting their own company, and so on. I have worked at agencies where if someone left for another agency, management took their departure as a personal affront. They would lash out verbally with snarky comments to those left behind. This behavior is unnecessary, unfortunate, and uncalled for.

I have also worked at agencies where management makes it a positive experience when a team member leaves. They understand that it's not necessarily a reflection on their agency or management style; rather, it's about the person who is leaving exploring a new experience.

Some agencies even have a revolving-door policy. I call this a Boomerang Program. They leave the door open for their personnel to come back if the job that they left for doesn't end up being all they hoped it would be. They allow their employee to go off and experience new things at a new job. If the new job doesn't live up to their expectations and there is still an opening, the agency allows the employee to come back. There are benefits for both parties involved with a Boomerang Program. For the employee, they are able to come back to a familiar place with friends and coworkers. For the agency, they get to fill an opening with someone who is experienced and doesn't have to be trained. It also helps support a fantastic office culture. When valued employees know that they can take a chance to explore another opportunity and return if it doesn't work out and there is still an opening, it helps elicit a sense of loyalty and security with the agency. (Big shout out to Frank Guerra, Beth Wammack, and Carey Quackenbush at GDC Marketing + Ideation in San Antonio for modeling their Boomerang Program! Check them out: www.gdc-co.com.)

## To Make Your Creatives More Capable

You want to have team members that are capable, not only as creatives, but as members of the agency/studio team as a whole. They should become familiar with the day-to-day business and the clients. With employee training and development, you are helping them grow into a stronger group that can handle more responsibility, which in turn results in a better creative product, improves communication between team members and clients, and frees you up to focus on other duties and responsibilities.

## To Keep Creatives Engaged

Bored creatives leave. Once they become disgruntled, they either end up leaving or producing poor work: plain and simple. They will become negative and sloppy and there is a very real possibility that their attitude and behavior will disrupt the overall team. Your investment in their development is a way to keep them engaged at work and help keep boredom or dissatisfaction from creeping in.

## To Save and Earn Money

Believe it or not, creatives that receive your regular training and have opportunities for development can save you money. They become more efficient and proficient with their skills and complete work assignments quicker and more accurately. This results in increased output, which is good for your bottom line. They are also a positive influence on other team members.

## Investing in Your Future

The time you put into team development has a definite impact on your level of success in the future. As you plan or develop a plan for creative team development, you should ask yourself several questions:

- What kind of leadership will I need to provide to my team?

- What will my clients need from their creative team?

- What does the agency need from the creative team?

- What will my creative team need from me?
- What industry changes are on the horizon?
- What can I do for my own professional development?

You must think ahead and determine what the answers to these questions are. You have to plan for the future because any development you'd like to provide for your creative team won't happen without it. Look at the opportunities that you are willing to put some of your budget into. Some of the technologies that are being taught and utilized today may not be the technologies of tomorrow. What do your creative team members want and need to learn?

Stay alert to comments made by your team. Often times, they will tell you what they feel they need without actively verbalizing it to you. If you really listen to them, you'll know what type of training they'd like to have. Keep ahead of the curve and show your creatives you are dedicated to their professional development.

# Motivating Your Creatives

When you motivate your creatives, you will find it has a snowball effect on the entire agency/studio. People talk. I guarantee, the processes and programs you put in place for your creative team will have a positive impact on the agency/ studio as a whole. The better each creative team member is, the better their output is, and the better the agency as a whole will be.

You want to cultivate a culture that inspires creativity. After all, that's what we're selling. When you do this, you will motivate your team members to offer a greater number of quality ideas and increase the team's chance for success. How do you do this?

- **Give timely and honest feedback on new ideas**. Idea generation takes time. It's not as it we have ideas floating around in our heads waiting to be released through a pressure-release idea valve. Your creative team needs to know their creativity is valued and they need opportunities to enhance their skills and nurture their creativity.

- **Reward collaboration.** You will notice that some of the best ideas start as a spark from one team member and are built on by others. Because creativity is an iterative process, your creative team members need to be motivated to work together. Acknowledge everyone involved in the process to encourage future teamwork and fuel creativity.

- **Celebrate well-considered failures.** Sometimes even the best ideas will fail. You need to be willing to take risks and push creative boundaries to reap the rewards of innovation. In all honesty, being creative involves taking a certain amount of risk. Creatives who play it safe are producing things that have worked for them in the past. That is one way to quickly get yourself replaced. If you want your team to take risks, you must motivate their creativity and reward well-thought-out ideas, even when they lead to failure. Sometimes less-than-stellar ideas lead to really great ones. Even if they don't, celebrate the effort. When you do, you send a message that you're rewarding the willingness to try and improve, and that taking risks is part of the creative process.

Knowing how to motivate employees is not easy. In your role as a creative leader, one of your most important tasks is to take care of your team and keep them in top creative form. By making this a priority, your team will continue to produce outstanding work and remain loyal to your agency/studio.

# In a Nutshell

How do I sum up this chapter? It's easy: Taking care of your creative teams is one of the best ways to guarantee success. You must ensure that they feel valued and appreciated or they can't do their best work. When you believe in and invest in them, their confidence and willingness to push the creative envelope during the creative process will increase.

As a creative leader, it's your task to keep your creative team motivated. When you can keep them motivated they will produce their best work. The way you do this is to show that you are willing to make investments in their professional development. Devote time to your team. From an altruistic standpoint, you can feel good that they will grow and develop their skills. From a selfish standpoint, knowing that you're making your creatives feel happy and valued will give you a warm, fuzzy feeling inside. Awww… Isn't that sweet?

# Don't Just Take It from Me

## What other creative leaders have to say

While compiling my notes and writing this book, I thought it would be beneficial to contact friends and colleagues who have made their way through the ranks to creative leadership and gather some insights from them. Because we have all taken different paths to leadership, I believe it's also important hear perspectives other than mine. As you read this chapter, you will discover a common thread— these leaders are passionate about their craft and driven to succeed.

Everyone in this chapter was provided with the same questions. They have chosen to respond to them in their own way. There were no requirements to how they responded or how many questions they answered.

As you read the words of Claudia Camargo (LatinWorks: Austin), Kim Arispe (POP: Seattle), Kevin Lane (Razorfish: Austin), Monica Ramirez Nadala (Geometry: Chicago), Lisette Sacks (New York), Elizabeth Grace Saunders, Jessica Walsh (Sagmeister & Walsh: New York), and Debbie Millman (Sterling Brands: New York), you may be even more inspired to succeed as a creative leader.

© Eleazar Hernández 2017
E. Hernández, *Leading Creative Teams*, DOI 10.1007/978-1-4842-2056-6_13

**Figure 13-1.** Maria Claudia Camargo

## Claudia Camargo

Art Director

LatinWorks: Austin, Texas

http://cargocollective.com/claudiacamargo/

www.latinworks.com

---

Born in Bogotá, Colombia, Claudia Camargo moved to the United States 16 years ago. The past eight years of her life have been devoted to advertising, and she would not have it any other way. Quickly becoming a hybrid of Hispanic and American cultures, now she considers Spanglish her first language. Claudia is an art director who is taking stabs at copywriting for fun. Her knowledge and experience come from working at some of the best Hispanic agencies such as Alma Advertising Agency in Miami, Florida and now LatinWorks in Austin, Texas. When it comes to her job, Claudia strives to discover and develop new ways to be creative while maintaining extreme focus on the Hispanic market.

---

**How long have you been in the industry?** I have been in advertising for seven years. My first job in advertising was as a Studio Artist while I was still in school.

**What type of degree do you have?** A Bachelor of Science in Advertising.

**What would be your dream job?** To be a creative director at an agency where there is a total 50/50 gender ratio.

**Describe your typical day.** I get to work and check e-mails. If I already know what I have to do, I jump on in. If I am not sure, I have a quick check in with my Creative Directors. I have to have a cup of green tea, otherwise I just don't function. I don't really have a set schedule because with a client like Target, you just never know what the day brings.

**How do you stay current in your knowledge and your skills?** I try to keep up with what's going on in the industry through blogs, websites, podcasts, conferences. But I also like to be very immersed in pop culture because that is where advertising comes from. I watch every single awards show, whether I like it or not. I also watch any new shows that are creating buzz. I keep up with music. Everything that shapes society as we know it, I like to follow closely.

**Do you have any formal supervisory/leadership training?** No, I have been lucky enough to be mentored by the three best creatives at LatinWorks. Everything I am now as a creative, I owe to them. With them I learn how the manage situations, clients, meetings, and teams every day. I try to absorb as much as I can.

**How do you deal with different creative personalities on your team?** Both of my Creative Directors are total polar opposites. That's probably why they have good chemistry. It's always fun to see them interact, get into arguments, laugh. I have learned to celebrate each person's strengths; whether I consider them a strength or not is a different story, but if they are good at what they do, who am I to judge?

**Did you have any mentors?** Still do and always will! My two Creative Directors and the Executive Creative Director at LatinWorks and a Creative Director from Alma. Not to say that all my peers have always played a huge role.

**What advice do you remember them sharing with you that you utilize or that holds true for you now?** To learn how to talk and interact with other people (accounts, client, peers). I have a very strong personality and I usually just say what I am thinking. I am still learning how to say what's on my mind without sounding careless. I believe I have found the perfect team that celebrates who I am and takes the time to shape me into a better creative without shutting me down.

**What advice would you give creatives who aspire to make it to creative director?** The advice that I give to my future self as a Creative Director is "don't be mean." Respect and fear are two very different things. I want to be a leader who guides, not a bossy bitch. Also, don't be a "know it all." Your creatives will have a fresher mind. Just because you have the experience doesn't mean that you do know it all.

***What warnings would you give?*** This is not an easy world. We live in a time of constant change. Be receptive to new things, especially what young talented creatives can bring to the table.

***Do you have any techniques for presenting that work particularly well?*** My Creative Directors taught me to write an outline or a script of what I am going to say. Go over it a couple of times and memorize key points. When I'm up there I end up improvising half of it, but being prepared beforehand does help.

***How do you brainstorm?*** I am a mess brainstorming because I get easily distracted. I like to read BuzzFeed while I brainstorm. I think is a great source of pop culture, fresh content and new ideas. I also like to see other ads or case studies. Sometimes, I just scroll through design blogs and it helps spark ideas. For websites of inspiration I always check Adfreak (for advertising), Creativity Online (for pop culture), BuzzFeed, Vice, Fusion, Flama, Remezcla (for design inspiration), VisualGraphc (yes, the spelling is correct).

***What role does research play in your brainstorms?*** *Huge!* Planners are your biggest allies. Granted, you still have to do your own research, but the bulk of it should come from your Planners, if you have them.

***Do you brainstorm in large groups or do you try to limit the number of people involved?*** I haven't had a partner for the past two years. At this point, I have gotten used to working on my own. I still enjoy brainstorming with some people, but I am very picky who I brainstorm with. I have to have a good vibe with that person.

**Figure 13-2.** Kim Arispe

## Kim Arispe

Senior Art Direction + Creative Leadership

Seattle, Washington

www.KimArispe.com

Kim Arispe is a senior art director and creative manager who leads teams in creating award-winning work in traditional and digital media for brands like Starbucks, Target, Procter & Gamble, Home Depot, H-E-B Grocery, Time Warner Cable, and the San Antonio Spurs. Her work has been recognized by the American Advertising Federation, Logo Lounge, Font Aid, the Aster Awards, and *HOW Design Magazine*. Kim enjoys battling it out at amateur "Iron Chef–style" cooking competitions and blogging about her passion for food, travel, and everyday moments. She is also currently working on her first cookbook.

*What does your job entail?* I lead a team of full-time and freelance art directors, designers, and copywriters. I oversee all work from initial client briefing to final execution. My responsibilities include guiding the work/team in brainstorms and internal reviews, partnering with strategist to write creative briefs, working closely with UX and content strategy, client presentations, scoping the work for timing and resources, account leadership and innovation (and being a therapist and scapegoat—that last one is not by choice).

*How do you distribute the work?* Every week I meet with my project managers and resourcing director to review the current and upcoming projects (sometimes up to 25 or more at a time) and make assignments. In our war room, we have a giant color-coded calendar grid displaying all projects, internal and client deadlines, resources/assigned hours, and internal and client out-of-office schedule. I assign people to projects based on their talent, experience/context from a similar past project. Basically, who is the best person for the work from my dedicated team. Then, my resourcing manager tells me all the reasons why I can't make those assignments based on other work or vacation time. This meeting is also where we decide if we need to hire more people to fill any gaps. It's like trading players in the NBA. Or, like playing Tetris at Level 10. And it happens every week, and goes on throughout the rest of the week as project timelines speed up or get put on hold.

*How do you deal with different creative personalities on your team?* I'm still figuring this one out! This is one of the hardest parts of my job. I'd say patience and over-communication is my go-to.

*What do you feel the biggest differences are between your previous creative experience and your current gig?* At GDC Marketing + Ideation and previous places, I was able to wear so many hats. You could say I filled the role of designer, art director, project manager, producer, interior designer, coordinator, strategist, UX designer, the list goes on. At POP, my role is more narrowly focused on creative work and team leadership. Also, a lot of agencies and corporations in Seattle have many contractors on their staff. It's just not something I'd ever experienced before.

**What was the transition from your previously print- and broadcast-heavy to your currently digitally focused job like?** I had already been leading the digital efforts at GDC, coordinating, producing, and designing websites and apps, so the transition wasn't too hard. Learning who to talk to when and who does what was the biggest challenge. You have all these roles like—Dev, IA, UX, QA, Motion, etc., etc. One of the things I learned from my time working on Target was accessibility standards. You have to make sure that your information is accessible to anyone with disabilities—that means any kind of vision, hearing, or cognitive impairment. Imagine a visually impaired person trying to scan a webpage and purchase a product. There are many rules around type sizes, colors, image tags, etc.

**Did your degree prepare you for what you're doing now?** Oh, hell no! I have learned through trial and error… lots of error.

**How did you prepare to take a leadership role?** When I first started at POP, I was on an established team and it was nothing but smooth sailing. After we won the Starbucks account, I became the lead creative and had one designer and writer. In less than a year, I grew the team to over 20 people. We didn't have a Creative Director or an Account Director, so it was me and my Senior Project Manager, Amy, just rolling up our sleeves and doing it all. We were so scrappy. It's like I woke up one day and had this giant team. I literally hired ten people in two days when we were super-busy at the end of last year. Design school never taught me how to interview people, let alone manager a team of creatives.

**Do you have any techniques for presenting work?** I've taken a couple of presentation classes and read a couple of books. I think the biggest thing I've learned is to be myself, and not try to mimic other great presenters. That, and 75% of what you say is actually "how" you say it and not "what" you say. If I am passionate about what I'm talking about, it will resonate with people, even if I don't always say all the "perfect" words.

**How do you stay current in your knowledge and your skills?** Great question. I feel like I've become a subject matter expert (SME) on all things Starbucks and on most loyalty programs. This has really been my focus. I like to dive really deep and learn everything I can about what makes a brand tick. I research other brands and also rely on my strategy team to supplement some specific target info.

**What advice do you remember your mentors sharing with you that you utilize or that holds true for you now?** One of the things that really resonated with me was the idea of making my team feel like I "have their back." One of my mentors said that to me, "No one can fault you if that is your main priority… fighting for your team and making sure they feel like you have their back." That really changed my perspective and I think it's great advice—above all people want to feel supported and understood.

*What is the hierarchy at POP (i.e., Junior Art Director, Art Director, Senior Art Director, etc.)?* The structure at POP is interesting. A lot of responsibility is assigned to each position. For instance, my job description and responsibilities as a Senior Art Director are comparable to a Creative Director in smaller agencies in Seattle or most agencies in San Antonio. Most of my day-to-day responsibilities revolve around creative direction and strategic thinking. To paint a better picture, I've hired creatives that had the title of Art Director (AD) in their previous agency and were given the title of Senior Designer at POP based on the responsibilities and experience that is required at POP. The hierarchy for design is: Designer, Senior Designer, Art Director, Senior Art Director, Associate Creative Director (ACD), Creative Director, Executive Creative Director (ECD) (there is only one ECD overseeing the whole creative department at POP, where other larger agencies might have an ECD over a certain part of the business, and then a Global Creative Director (GCD) overseeing everything). For writers, it goes copywriter, senior copywriter, ACD, CD.

**Figure 13-3.** Kevin Lane

**Kevin Lane**

Associate Creative Director

Razorfish: Austin, Texas

www.razorfish.com

---

When Kevin was a kid filling in the Sunday morning crossword, his grandmother taught him that words equal ideas. He has been playing with syllables and stories ever since. For the past nine years, he has been making groundbreaking advertising with amazing brands and incredible people. He has worked on commercials, interactive print ads, and even tweeted bikes. As a leader, Kevin focuses on inspiring creatives of all types. He also enjoys driving the business side of things from client goals to agency operations. He believes his biggest strength is his ability to always bring tacos. Off the clock, you'll find him traveling with his lady, running his YouTube channel, or killing a crossword.

---

**Is this the first time you've been a creative lead?** Yes, I recently made the jump to leadership. I've been ACD for about six months now.

**What was your first creative job and how long did it take you to get to your current position?** I started out on a two-week trial run as a junior copywriter. I failed miserably, but I think they just needed a warm body, so somehow I got the gig. I've been in advertising ever since, for almost nine years now.

**What would be your dream job?** What I'm doing now—leading creative on an iconic brand (Patrón) as part of a fully integrated team. I love working on a brand that has a rich history of heritage and craft. I also love doing integrated work, and we work with other agencies who handle the traditional, social, PR, retail, and events work for Patrón. All the agencies work really well together, and that makes the work we all do even better.

**What is the hierarchy at your current location (i.e., Junior Art Director, Art Director, Senior Art Director, etc.)?**

- Jr. Copywriter to Copywriter to Sr. Copywriter to ACD to CD

- Jr. Designer to Designer to Sr. Designer to Art Director to Sr. AD to ACD to CD

I know it seems like there are more steps for art, but you usually spend longer in each role as a writer, so it all pretty much evens out.

**What are your favorite projects?** My favorite projects are where all the pieces come together perfectly, and business gets done. That first part never really happens, but that's the fun part. And if the business goals are met, everyone goes home even happier. Motorola, #UseMeLeaveMe, and Patrón are my three favorites to date.

**What was your role in the creation of those projects?** For Motorola, I concepted the creative campaign and messaging—I also learned how to program a computer to read colors, but I couldn't do it for you today. On #UseMeLeaveMe, I helped conceive the stunt, wrote a personality for 20 bikes, and soldered together the brains of each bike. On Patrón, I've led product launches, a 360° mobile experience, a mobile-first redesign, and their latest Margarita of the Year campaign.

**Do you produce work, lead a team to produce the work, or both?** Occasionally I jump in and produce work, but I try to stay out of the way by leading instead of doing.

**What does your job entail?** Team kickoffs and check-ins, client presentations, agency-to-agency relations, mentorship, learning, paperwork, and making stuff up. Best job ever.

**Describe your typical day.**

- 9–10am Coffee, hellos, emails, daily planning
- 10–10:30am Team stand-up (assignments, check-ins, housecleaning, updates)
- 10:30–11am Client check-in (status, updates, housecleaning)
- 11am–12pm Individual check-ins with team, prep for upcoming presentation
- 12–1pm Lunch with team or other colleagues
- 1pm–2pm Client presentation
- 2–2:15pm Coffee break, walk around the block, check on my team
- 2:15–3pm Team kickoff on a new project
- 3–4pm Agency-to-agency meeting to align on an ongoing project
- 4–5pm Prep for upcoming presentations
- 5–5:30pm Individual check-ins with team
- 5:30–6pm Emails
- 6pm Beer

**What do you feel the biggest differences are between any previous creative experience and your current position?** It sounds cliché, but leadership requires a lot more responsibility—time management, priority management, decision-making, team morale, business acumen, strategic thinking, and a little thicker skin. I used to only feel responsible for my own work, but now I feel responsible for my whole team's work, plus making sure everyone's happy with the work and the results—from clients to bosses to colleagues to consumers. It's been a big shift in thinking and doing, but I find it rewarding, thrilling, and just the right amount of scary.

**How do you stay current in your knowledge and your skills?** I'm always reading agency news, world news, and tech news. I try to meet other successful people and steal as much from their brains as I can. The occasional freelance or art project keeps me sharp as well.

**Do you have any formal supervisory/leadership training?** No formal training here, but I have a history of leading groups – from the theater troupe I was in in high school, to the band I started in college, to the startups I've helped with on the side.

**If not, how did you gain supervisory/leadership experience?** Even from a young age, the schools and clubs and bands and businesses I've been in... I've always been a natural leader. Through those experiences, I've learned how to get to know people, encourage them, and get out of their way so they can do amazing things.

**How do you deal with different creative personalities on your team?** I try to treat everyone the same but different. Different people respond to different stimuli, so I like to get to know everyone as much as possible so I know what they like to work on and what perspectives they bring and how they like to work – plus how to factor those things into the overall team/work equation. But if you're an asshole, I don't deal with you at all.

**What type of degree do you have?** Bachelor's of Science in Business Administration, with a dual focus in Marketing and Management from Trinity University.

**Did your degree plan prepare you for what you're doing now? If so, how? If not, how did you prepare for your current position?** Yes and no. It overprepared me for the business and management side of things. It didn't prepare me much at all for the creative side of things, but I was lucky enough to have life experiences and a natural hunger that made up for that.

**Did you learn on the job or were you prepared before taking the role?** A little of both. I've always been a creative writer, so I had the raw talent before. But all the advertising stuff I definitely learned on the job.

**What advice do you remember your mentors sharing with you that you utilize or that holds true for you now?** Oh man, a lot. They've given me all kinds of creative, strategy, and business wisdom, as well as great advice in life, love, and happiness. The biggest lessons they've taught me have been to keep it simple, choose your battles, dole out credit, never stop learning, fight for your people, listen more than you talk, and the art of the soft sell.

**Do you mentor any younger creatives?** I do. I'm always there for my team and colleagues. And even when people I don't know reach out, I make myself available and offer any advice or help that I can.

**What advice would you give other creative directors or creatives who aspire to make it to creative director?** I always go with Garrison Keillor's signoff from The Writer's Almanac: "Be well, do good work, and keep in touch." Be well, because if you're not physical and mentally healthy, your work is going to suffer. Do good work, because when you're proud of the things you create, it drives you to make your next project even better. And keep in touch, because the ad world is all about connections, and most people are always willing to help.

**What warnings would you give?**

- If you don't love advertising, get out. Life's too short to do something that doesn't make you happy.

- Don't be an asshole. You're better than that.

- Don't fall in love with your ideas. A lot of them are going to die on the cutting room floor. If you had a great idea today, you'll have another one tomorrow.

- Learn the business side of things. It'll make your ideas stronger, your clients happier, and your work more effective.

- Raise your hand. The most successful creatives are those that aren't afraid to take on extra work and "small" assignments. You'll get more work out in the world, and you'll get an even cooler project next time.

**Do you present your work to clients?** Yes, everything from minor updates to fully integrated campaigns. Most are over the phone, but many are also in person. And the occasional pitch.

**Do you have any techniques for presenting that you believe work particularly well?** The best technique I've learned is to slow down. The goal is not to get through every slide; the goal is to start a conversation.

**How do you brainstorm? Are there any techniques you use or find particularly useful?** Whiteboard all day. When you're spitballing ideas, it helps to get them all out and up on the board. That way everyone can see their contribution, come back to an idea later, and not be afraid to blurt random things out. Once everything is up, I like to bucket ideas under themes to see what's working, what's not, and where the holes are. Then we do a one-sheeter on each idea—a representative image/sketch and a short writeup (three sentences max). Eventually the best ideas stick around and start to work together, while the not-so-great ones fall away.

*What role does research play in your brainstorms?* A ton. Every big assignment starts with consumer research by our planners, who will do focus groups and follow-alongs and in-home interviews. They also tap into trends, demographics, and research studies. Then they distill all that down into a few key insights, which the creative department will play off of. I find the research part crucial, because it gives you that nugget of truth that can make an idea personal yet universal.

*Do you sketch before going to the computer?* I do. Even though I'm a writer, I like to sketch things out. And most of the designers and art directors I know like to sketch things out first. I think it's because it lets you get a lot of ideas out quickly, and it helps you distill things down to their simplest form.

*Do you brainstorm in groups or do you try to limit the number of people involved?* I like small teams—five people max. If there's a large group, I like to split off into smaller groups. It helps you find chemistry quicker and feel less afraid to speak up.

**Figure 13-4.** Monica Ramirez Nadala

## Monica Ramirez Nadela

Creative Director

Geometry Global. Multicultural Practice: Chicago, Illinois

https://geometry.com

Monica has over ten years of experience in designing on-strategy, on-target, and on-budget cross-platform marketing solutions in the following categories: Retail, CPG/Beverage, QSR, Technology & Telecommunications. Some of the clients she has worked with are Tecate, US Army, Nextel, JCPenney, MillerCoors, ConAgra Foods, JMS Smucker's, Hershey's, Kraft, H-E-B, Amway, Kimberly-Clark, Jim Beam, Liberty Mutual, and Mondelēz.

*Creative Mantra:* Think Action. Inspire Action. *Connect.* Never stop asking why? Solve a need. Make it different. Earn loyalty. Win hearts and a place in their carts. Preserve meaningful connections.

*Persona:* Culture & Insight Matchmaker. Heart & Head Idea Advocate. Strategic Adjudicator. Creative Solutionist. Brand Whisperer. Processes Championer. Results Deliverer. Turnaround Driver. Bicultural Explorer. Spanish, English and Spanglish Adventurer.

*Journey:* My work on both the agency and client side focuses on building solutions at the intersection of the brand and sales objectives. For more than 15 years I've been exploring and unveiling the fascinating Hispanic Market. As a foreign-born U.S. Hispanic, I've ridden the acculturation roller coaster through the diverse stages, absorbing and applying all the knowledge and learning into my work. Today, I'm still riding it and I'm having fun learning!

*What led you toward your current position of creative director?* When I started working in advertising, I don't believe I had set my mind on becoming a Creative Director, I think what took me down this path was my passion for communicating and engaging with people. Since I was in college back in Mexico City, my passion always was more about the content and the people than the mediums or methods.

*What was your first creative job and how long did it take you to get to your current position?* My first "official" job in an agency was as a Junior Spanish Copywriter, which was back in 2001. Roughly, it took me about 15 years to get here, but I think every Creative Director's story is different and there is no such thing as a "standard" number of years you need to pay your dues to become a CD. I believe what it takes to be a CD is *drive*, not time.

*What would be your dream job?* That's a tough question! I think my dream job changes as I grow older, but in all the versions of my "dream job" it's about connecting and engaging with people, it involves design and art, but above all, it's about something that adds value to your life.

*What is the hierarchy at your current location (i.e., Junior Art Director, Art Director, Senior Art Director, etc.)?* We have art and copy, then Senior Art and Copy, Associate Creative Director (which can come from any background), Creative Director, Group Creative Director, and our Executive Creative Directors.

**Describe your typical day.** Every day is very different, but I spend a lot of time meeting with planners, creative directors, and account directors to drive the creative strategy, attend brainstorms, and do some work, a lot of research and writing opinion pieces. There's a lot of work before we get to execution and every brand has different timings. Every day is different, there's no routine, except for getting to the office.

**What do you feel the biggest differences are between any previous creative experience and your current position?** The biggest difference is the support I have received from the organization; they empower me to share my knowledge and my vision and to sharpen my skills. Training is another big difference, access to tools and mentorship is key in this agency, and last but not least is how everyone works: as a team, and of course the teams here are quite larger than what I was used to back in Texas. (In a brainstorm session you can have anywhere from 10 to 20 brilliant creative minds!)

**How do you stay current in your knowledge and your skills?** Subscriptions to the top industry publications, newsletters, etc.; key conferences, reading, reading, searching, searching, and observing! Always learning from senior and junior people.

**Do you have any formal supervisory/leadership training?** No. When I first became an Associate Creative Director I probably made a lot of mistakes but I took it upon myself to look for inspiration on creative director blogs, reading books, taking personality assessments and training when they were available. Nowadays I'm very fortunate to have access to tools to learn and the guidance of my mentors and my boss.

**How do you deal with different creative personalities on your team?** It's a learning process, but to me, the most important element is respect. You have to respect every member of your team in order to establish a relationship and be able to figure out what is going to work for both parties. While creating a list of tasks might work for one of your team members, you might be better to give another one more responsibility. As the lead of your team you need to understand their strengths and weaknesses in order to help them grow. When differences arise between your team, your role is to be the mediator and remain neutral while reminding them what is at task and what to focus energy on. I personally like to talk to each team member in private about the conflict to try to understand what originated it and try to find a solution.

**Do you have a degree?** I graduated in Mexico City from a Licenciatura en Comunicación con especialidad en Filosofía, which roughly equates in the U.S. to a Bachelor's Degree in Fine Arts with a major in Philosophy

**Did your degree plan prepare you for what you're doing now?** To a certain degree, yes. My studies were really more focused on the contents of the communications; how to connect with people by understanding what drives and makes them tick, a lot about how ideas are generated, psychology, sociology, etc. We did also have the technical part of how to produce radio, TV, movies, and how to design and craft an advertising campaign. All that was very useful.

*Did you have any mentors?* I do now. I was looking for them for a long time, and I finally found them here at Geometry.

*What advice have they shared with you that you utilize or that holds true for you now?* From the creative prospective, it is about how the ideas we create should change behaviors, what is "that thing" that will make people change and act. From the leadership role is to not to become a shell that is so focused on her responsibilities and deliverables, but to be with the rest of the creatives and feed of their fresh thinking and energy.

*What advice would you give other creative directors or creatives who aspire to make it to creative director?* [They taught me that] being a Creative Director is not about the "shiny" title, but more about the commitment that you have with consumers to create ideas with passion and honesty.

*What warnings would you give?* It's a tough job. Some days you're completely drained. Any creative job is quite challenging. You need to keep yourself motivated, inspired and find a method that works for you to create ideas... Most of the times you can't wait for inspiration to strike because of timelines and due dates. So as a creative, you're responsible for keeping your mind clear, focused, and full of ideas at the same time, because you want to be able to do what is best for the idea at all times... My big red warning: you will be working 24/7... maybe not physically by being at the office (perhaps) but because solutions or ideas might come to you in the middle of your sleep (keep a recorder or notepad handy at your nightstand), in the shower (waterproof notepad, great gift from a colleague) or while you commute to work... It really never stops.

*Do you have any techniques for presenting that you believe work particularly well?* I'm a bit of a nerd, I do like to prepare before my presentations, commit the content I'm presenting to heart. I do not like to read off a PowerPoint. I like to create stories to present creative work and use images rather than words. Connecting with the audience before you start presenting is key (which is a bit challenging for me since I'm quite an introvert).

*How do you brainstorm?* Before I brainstorm with the team, I like to sit down with the planner and the account team to have crystal clear what the strategy we need to solve creatively is. After that, I like for the creatives to spend some time with it for initial thoughts. Once we have the brainstorm, the rule is there's no such a thing as bad ideas, everything goes on the board. Sometimes I like to use phrases as "what if"... to spark ideas, or write a list with words that are related to the task and start making associations. I don't have one "proven" method for brainstorm, you need to feel the energy of the group and adjust accordingly.

***What role does research play in your brainstorms?*** *Huge!!!!* You can't resolve a problem if you don't know the problem and its parts.

***Do you brainstorm in groups or do you try to limit the number of people involved?*** Both; I think it depends of the task at hand. For new big ideas, I like to have as many creatives, planners, and account people as possible at the first brainstorm, and then you regroup and follow the thinking process with a smaller group.

**Figure 13-5.** Lisette Sacks

## Lisette Sacks
Creative Director

New York

www.lisettesacks.com

---

Lisette Sacks has 17 years of experience in advertising and publishing: first as a graphic designer and the last nine years as a creative director and art director leading teams. She has deep Consumer Package Goods (CPG) expertise and a broad client portfolio spanning food, beauty, finance, and home.

Sacks has launched global brand campaigns in digital and print; social media content + campaigns, websites, video games and video content for American Express, American Greetings, Amway, Betty Crocker, Bisquick, Black Dinah Chocolatiers, Chex Mix, Cinnamon Toast Crunch, Dupont, Marzetti, MasterCard, Moen, Nature Valley, Nestlé, Sherwin Williams, Steinway & Sons, and Zing Zang.

---

***Have you always been on a path toward creative director?*** I started off as a graphic designer. For the first few years I never thought about my personal trajectory upward. I was interested in having fun and learning as much as I could. I have been very fortunate to have interned and worked in places that showed me different aspects of being a designer. At a boutique letterpress and design shop, Purgatory Pie Press's Dikko Faust taught me about typography in a way I never would have learned if I hadn't actually got my hands dirty setting type and working the letterpress. I've worked at multiple magazines, including *Wired* (where I interned) and was exposed to a much more rigorous attention to templates, grids, and pixel-perfect computer-based work in a Swiss aesthetic.

Conversely, I worked at American Greetings as a card designer where expression and free-form creativity off the computer was very much encouraged. I worked with top-notch calligraphers, illustrators, and photographers and got to see how they worked every day, which informed how I work with artists today.

I started doing web design work and animation in 1998. That led me to moving from design shops to advertising, where I never thought I'd end up, but which was a great place to tell stories, rather than just make things pretty. I became much more interested in copy, which was natural since I am a total book nerd and I am in awe of great copywriters. Advertising felt like I was finally using a lot of the parts of my brain that I hadn't when I was just doing design.

***What was your first creative job and how long did it take you to get to your current position?*** Aside from my internships, I was hired as a junior designer at a small (now defunct) design firm called Tieken Design. It was about a 15-person shop run by a husband and wife in Phoenix. It was all print design where I led my first photoshoot. That was 1996 and I was 26. I made $21,000 a year and I felt like I won the lottery back then. It took me 10 years to become a Creative Director moving up through various jobs.

***What led you to consulting and freelance?*** I worked at big and small boutique ad agencies throughout the country and finally became a Creative Director under the best mentor I ever had, the co-owner and Creative Director, Leslie Perls, at LP&G in Tucson, AZ. After a couple years there, she encouraged me to move to New York and try my hand "with the big boys." I was hesitant at first but I knew I'd never truly be happy with my career if I didn't *try* to make it in New York. Two months after her suggestion, I sold everything I owned and moved to NYC in 2009. After 6 months of no one wanting to talk to me, Doug Speidel the ECD, gave me a big break in New York at MRM / McCann—then the digital arm of McCann-Erickson. I became the CD of MasterCard and General Mills—working on Betty Crocker, Cinnamon Toast Crunch, and a bunch of other brands. I left after 3 1/2 years to freelance and work on my own. I now consult directly for brands and take occasional in-house freelance gigs.

*What would be your dream job?* Doing Creative Direction for a fashion brand.

*Are you primarily print focused, digitally focused, or a little of both?* I am mostly digital focused these days, including social media content and strategy, but I also do some packaging and print as part of the larger campaign.

*What do you do in a typical day?* I start work around 9am, read my feed of blogs (I use Feedly to aggregate everything I'm interested in) before I start my day, just to get a jolt of news and creative inspiration and to stay on top of trends. I then respond to e-mails. I check in with my team on various projects and that usually informs what needs to be done for the day. Sometimes I go straight into designing, sometimes I'm researching and creating a sort of inspiration brain dump, and then sometimes I'm actually concepting with my writing partner. It all depends on the project at hand. At some points I'm off the computer writing and taking notes. Oh, and in between all of that are meetings, meetings, meetings, which disrupt everyone's workflow but are the necessary evil to include members outside the creative team. I usually end work around 6:30 or 7pm or often later when the project calls for it.

*What do you feel the biggest differences are between any previous creative experience and your current position?* Freelancing really means being organized and holding oneself and one's team accountable for deliverables and timelines. It requires a lot of self-control to not get sucked down into rabbit holes on the Internet when researching. I feel like a project manager, account person, and creative director all rolled into one; whereas when I was working at firms or agencies those roles belonged to other people.

*How do you stay current in your knowledge and your skills?* I read a lot of design, tech blogs, news, and books on design and consumer consumption theory. I think there is something to learn every day. Listening to UX people and developers has really changed how I think about the creative process digitally. I also think it's very important to always hire people smarter or who think completely differently than you. People who work outside the industry are often excellent resources for new ideas. I have learned so much from people I've hired over the years.

*How did you gain supervisory/leadership experience?* I have been fortunate to have had some (aforementioned) great bosses. I learned by watching how they nurtured, supported, and created a great working culture. I always strive to create the environments that I thrived in when I was younger. Also by seeing that everyone is an individual. My management style adapts to the individual.

**When you supervise a team, how do you distribute the work?** I'm pretty democratic about workload. There are certain projects that I know will be great for certain people because they have experience in that specific market or a lot of interest or great skills. Sometimes, it's just the opposite—I might give work to someone who may not think they can do it, but I know they need to be pushed a little to show them that they can rock it if they believe in themselves a bit because I believe in their ability.

**How do you deal with different creative personalities on your team?** There's been a lot of difference in my teams. Sometimes it's age and experience, sometimes it's how they like to work. Sometimes it's shyness versus boldness in personality. A good manager should really know their teams and take everything into account and talk to people as individuals. Some people need more encouragement and check-ins and others need to be left alone to work independently. The main thing is really to understand each person's style and adapt. (It isn't always easy but it makes for better work in the end.)

**What type of degree do you have?** Bachelor of Fine Arts, Graphic Design. School gave me the basics of design and theory, but it did not show me how to manage or lead.

**How did you prepare for your creative leadership?** By watching and taking note of my own Creative Directors as I worked my way up to this role. I saw who I didn't want to be and I saw who I really wanted to emulate.

**Did you learn on the job or were you prepared before taking the role?** I think with every role I've had, I'm always biting off a little more than I can chew in the beginning (which is scary and exhilarating) and then I learn as I go and eventually it becomes second nature.

**Any advice from mentors that you utilize or that holds true for you now?** Not quite a mentor, but my professor (and Eleazar's), Louis Ocepek said once in a creative critique in school, "There is elegance in restraint." That has stuck with me and I think about it often. The best mentors like Leslie Perls and Cheryl Van Ooyen showed me that creating a nurturing environment, staying calm, and having a sense of humor when it seems everything is going array, is something I try my best to employ. (I often fail at staying calm, to my own dismay.)

**Do you mentor any younger creatives?** I am often asked to review portfolios, give advice, and help younger creatives. I am very honored and humbled to do so. I think this is the natural progression of being a Creative Director and I take it very seriously. I've noticed young women doubt themselves a lot and they need someone to embolden them and tell them it's okay if they haven't figured it all out yet. They just need to keep persevering. I'm very interested in helping younger women find their voice and encourage them to work towards being a CD. There need to be more women in advertising in leadership roles.

**What advice would you give other creative directors or creatives who aspire to make it to creative director?** To other creative directors: Work hard, be nice, and try to remember you were once in a lower position. Your ideas are not always the best ideas either. Keep learning and listen to people who work for you.

To aspiring creative directors: Work hard, educate yourself outside the field of design, look for inspiration in unexpected places (not just design or advertising), and fill your brain up with everything you can. You *never* know when it might come in handy. Read and look.

**What warnings would you give?** Don't be cocky or get too comfortable.

**Do you have any techniques for presenting that you believe work particularly well?** I have a love/hate relationship with presenting. In order to make it run smoothly I do a few things:

Prior to the day of the presentation, I outline my thoughts. I make notes (sometimes in Keynote) so I know what I want to touch on in each slide. I also do mini-rehearsals with the team if it is a big presentation. I like to be ready for client questions so I play Devil's advocate in my head and try to jot questions and answers down to what I imagine their concerns might be.

Once I'm in the room, I am a little bit jokey with the client. I keep things professional, but I also like to lighten the mood. There's a lot of tension sometimes in presentations but this is creative work and it should be fun. Listening and asking questions works well for me. I never want to leave a presentation where the client didn't feel heard when giving feedback.

**What role does research play in your brainstorms?** Research (and understanding the strategy and demographic) is the biggest thing before even beginning brainstorming for me. I am a stickler for a very well-written brief too.

**Do you sketch before going to the computer?** Sometimes I sketch but more often I write little notes to myself about combinations of ideas to evoke a certain mood or color or structure or to remember a feeling. A lot of my notes are about tapping into an emotion.

**Do you brainstorm in groups or do you try to limit the number of people involved?** Group brainstorming is great when it is structured and I have a certain technique for that so that it's not just everyone talking on top of each other. One-on-one brainstorming is faster and when it is someone you've worked with for a while, you know their style. When it's good, ideas just flow. Some of those "darlings" will get killed but every once in awhile, there's a great little angel that makes it to the campaign.

**Figure 13-6.** Elizabeth Grace Saunders

## Elizabeth Grace Saunders

Real Life E Founder, CEO

http://reallifee.com

---

Elizabeth Grace Saunders is the founder and CEO of Real Life E, a time coaching company that empowers individuals who feel guilty, overwhelmed, and frustrated to feel peaceful, confident, and accomplished. She is an expert on achieving more success with less stress. Real Life E also encourages Christians to align themselves with God's heart through Divine Time Management.

McGraw-Hill published Saunders' first book *The 3 Secrets to Effective Time Investment: How to Achieve More Success with Less Stress*. Harvard Business Review published her second book, *How to Invest Your Time Like Money*. Elizabeth contributes to blogs like Harvard Business Review, Forbes, Fast Company, and the 99U blog on productivity for creative professionals and has appeared on CBS, ABC, NBC, and Fox.

---

*You have written about creative leadership for 99U. Are there any tips that you can provide that would help guide creatives who want to achieve success at the higher levels of leadership?* When you move to a creative director role, you need to realize that your focus must shift from doing to leading. That means more time spent on planning work, communicating vision, giving feedback, and developing staff. Given that higher level of people management, you'll need to reduce your expectations around how much project work you can do yourself. If you don't, you'll end up frustrated because you'll end up working two jobs and not feel like you're doing a great job at either.

*As a leader, communication with the people you work with is a key component. What would you say is the most important things new leaders need to remember about communicating with their people?* As noted above, you do need to make time for communication. However, you also need to set boundaries and expectations. That means talking about your preferred method of communication, i.e., is email best or do you prefer other methods like IM or Slack. It also means discussing the most effective way to communicate to minimize interruptions. That could mean a daily stand-up to address the main questions for the day so that there are minimal drive by meetings or setting—and keeping—a weekly one-on-one with your direct reports.

*Embracing a new role is difficult. It can be even more difficult if you have suddenly moved to management over a team that was once your contemporaries. How would you recommend that new creative leaders go about preparing themselves and their new team or their new role?* Leading is about serving so starting out by meeting with each staff member one on one and understanding what support they need from you to thrive is critical. However, at the same time, you'll need to reset expectations on items that you will not do anymore given your new management responsibilities. That could include stepping off certain projects and/or delegating more. This allows you to spend more time giving direction and feedback across a broader range of work.

*For new creative leaders thrust into a management position, do you have any warnings for them? Anything they should watch out for?* Make sure that you still reserve time for the work that you do need to do. That could mean blocking out certain times of day or setting aside some larger blocks of time on multiple days. That could also mean working from home, a coffee shop, or ducking into a conference room when there's something really important that you need to focus on. Just because you're a manager doesn't mean that you always need to be available on demand.

**Figure 13-7.** Jessica Walsh

## Jessica Walsh

Designer + Art Director

New York: Sagmeister & Walsh

www.sagmeisterwalsh.com

Jessica Walsh is a designer and art director working in New York City. She is a partner at the New York–based design studio Sagmeister & Walsh. She teaches at the School of Visual Arts and speaks internationally about design and creativity. Her work has won awards from most design competitions including Type Director's Club, Red Dot, Art Director's Club, SPD, D&AD, Print, and Graphis. Her work has also been featured in numerous books, magazines, and exhibitions. She has also received various celebrated distinctions such as *Forbes'* "30 under 30 greatest makers" *Computer Arts'* "Top Rising Star in Design," an Art Director's Club "Young Gun," and *Print Magazine*'s "New Visual Artist." Clients include Jay Z, Barneys, Museum of Modern Art, The Jewish Museum, *The New York Times*, Levis, Adobe, and The School of Visual Arts.

***What is your creative philosophy?*** I am interested in creating emotionally engaging, concept-driven work that is embodied in beautiful forms. I always try to approach the process in a playful way, with a sense of humor. I want people who view my work to experience or feel something, whether it makes them think, brings them joy, or offers them inspiration. I always aim to create functional work that achieves our clients' goals.

***Where do you find inspiration?*** I believe that creativity is all about making interesting connections between things that already exist. I think inspiration for those connections can come from everything we experience as human beings: our conversations, our travels, our dreams, art, a great psychology book, our love lives, etc. I try not to look within our own field of design for inspiration; that's when you run the risk of regurgitating styles and techniques people are used to seeing. If you find your inspirations from unexpected places, and vary your inspirations to not be too close to any one source, it's easier to create unique work. I frequent museums and shows and look at all kinds of creative work, like fashion, furniture design, painting, photography, and sculpture. I listen to music and have conversations with friends. I read books about psychology and science, and blogs about popular culture. The list goes on.

***Do you avoid trends?*** Trendy design and styles can work if you are designing something temporary, like an illustration in a magazine or a poster with a short lifespan. However, most of the time at our studio, we seek to create work that can have a long lifespan and stay relevant for a long while, especially in relation to branding. The identity and visual language we create for our clients should stay fresh and relevant even after a decade.

***Do you have any techniques for presenting that you believe work particularly well for you?*** We only show our client one option. We've found that it's much harder to force ourselves to think of the best possible solution to a client's problem based on their goals, brand personality, and restrictions (timelines, budgets). It's easy for us to come up with five possible solutions and let the client decide; however, this often leads to mediocre work. When you show options, the client often ends up picking and choosing their favorite parts of the various options like a buffet and all of a sudden you end up with a "frankencomp" which you never meant to happen. This isn't good for us or our clients.

The technique of forcing ourselves to really study and immerse ourselves in our client's product/culture, understand their goals, and then come up with a smart single solution that we know will work well for them, has worked well for us. Most of our best work has come out of this method. We do assure our clients that if they don't like our presentation, we'll completely redo it. However, when we spend so much time and strategy in the initial presentation phase as we do, we most often do create things our clients like.

**How do clients react to only one design option when the industry is accustomed to multiple options?** We assure our clients that if they don't like what we do, we'll redo it. However our clients are usually happy with what we create. I believe a large part of this is due to the enormous time we spend on research and process. We strategize with our clients to determine brand personality attributes, which our work will then reflect. We research their target audience and do competitive analysis. We force ourselves to think of the best possible solution for a client that is also respectful of their budgets and restrictions. It is much harder to come up with one great idea than it is to come up with numerous iterations and make the client decide. This does not make things easier for us. However, we have found that it yields better results.

**How do you deal with client rejection?** We try to listen to them and understand exactly why it isn't working for them. If we agree that there is something we can do that will function better for them, we'll revise the work.

**Are there any techniques you use to brainstorm?** Try making unexpected connections between things. So thinking of random words or nouns and then thinking about how they can connect to the project you are designing for.

**Who are your role models?** I truly believe that you can learn something from almost anyone. I know that no one person is perfect, and often when a person excels greatly in one aspect of life, another aspect suffers. I've never been a "fan" or "starstruck" of anyone because of this. Instead I look up to and admire certain qualities from all different kinds of people. If I have to list a few off the top of my head right now: my mom, Alain de Botton, my cleaning lady, Salvador Dalí, Walt Disney, Albert Einstein, my sister, Charles Bukowski. In the design industry, I am inspired by those who are not just strong formally but also author their own projects and have a unique voice: Christoph Niemann, Maira Kalman, Stefan Sagmeister, Paul Sahre, Brian Rae, Tibor Kalman, and Timothy Goodman, among many others.

**Figure 13-8.** Debbie Millman

## Debbie Millman

Chief Marketing Officer

Sterling Brands: New York, London, San Francisco, Chicago

www.sterlingbrands.com

---

Named "one of the most influential designers working today" by *Graphic Design: USA*, Debbie Millman is also an author, educator, brand strategist, and host of the podcast Design Matters. As the founder and host of Design Matters, the first and longest-running podcast about design, Millman has interviewed more than 250 design luminaries and cultural commentators, including Massimo Vignelli, Milton Glaser, Malcolm Gladwell, Dan Pink, Barbara Kruger, Seth Godin, and more. In the 11 years since its inception, the show has garnered over a million downloads per year, a Cooper Hewitt National Design Award, and—most recently—iTunes designated it one of the best podcasts of 2015.

Debbie is the author of six books and two collections of illustrated essays. Her artwork has been exhibited at the Chicago Design Museum, Anderson University, School of Visual Arts, Long Island University, and The Wolfsonian Museum.

Debbie is the Chief Marketing Officer at Sterling Brands, where she has worked with over 200 of the world's largest brands, including the redesign of Burger King, merchandising for *Star Wars,* and the positioning and branding of the No More movement. She is also President Emeritus of AIGA, one of five women to hold the position in the organization's 100-year history and a past board member and treasurer of the New York chapter. She has been a juror for competitions including Cannes Lions, The Art Directors Club, The Type Directors Club, *Fast Company, HOW Magazine, Print Magazine, ID Magazine,* AIGA, The Dieline, and more. Currently, Debbie is the editorial and creative director of *Print Magazine,* the oldest magazine about design in the United States.

---

**Could you give a little insight into your ideas on creative leadership in terms of your career trajectory?** My love affair with brands began when I was in the seventh grade. I looked around and everyone in school was wearing really cool pants with a little red tag on the back pocket and polo shirts with little crocodiles on the front right section over your heart. Levi's and Lacoste. But they were expensive and my mother didn't understand why we had to pay more money for the little red tag and the crocodile when clothing without them was the same quality, only cheaper. Furthermore, she was a seamstress and her compromise to me was an offer to make me the very same clothes and stitch a red tag into the back pocket of the pants and glue a crocodile patch from the Lee Wards craft store onto the front of a perfectly good polo shirt from Modell's. While that plan didn't quite suit my aspirations of being a seventh-grade trendsetter or at least voted the best-dressed girl at Elwood Junior High, I eagerly pored through the racks of Lee Wards desperately searching for a crocodile patch to stick onto the front of my favorite pink polo shirt. Alas, there were none. Nothing even close. The best I came up with was a cute rendition of Tony the Tiger, but that really wasn't the brand look I was going for.

I rode my bike home from Lee Wards dejected and mopey and when mom found out I wasn't successful, I could see she felt sorry for me. She then took the matter into her own hands. The Lacoste shirts were too expensive, but there were indeed some Levi's on sale at the Walt Whitman Mall and she bought me a pair. Problem was she didn't get me the denim kind like everyone else was wearing, she found me a pair that must of been from the triple mark-down racks... they were a pair of lime green corduroy bell-bottom Levi's. It was with a mixture of horror and pride that I paraded in front of the full-length mirror in my bedroom, ever-so-slightly sticking my butt out so that I could be sure the little red tag would show. So what, I was wearing lime green corduroy! They were Levi's. I was cool. My reign of logo worship had begun.

Logos and brands are not the only things I love. From the time I was child, I loved to make things. I made my own coloring books, I made my own paper dolls, I made dioramas, and I even tried to make my own perfume by crushing rose petals into baby oil. I made barrette boxes out of Popsicle sticks, key chains out of lanyards, ashtrays out of clay and Halloween costumes out of construction paper and old sheets. I even handmade an entire magazine when I was 12 with my best friend. Her name was Debbie also and we named the magazine *Debutante*. We were very proud of it.

I went to the State University at Albany in New York. I had an incredible education, despite the lack of fancy pedigree. I knew I wanted to do something creative but thought I was going to be a painter. I studied painting and took some design classes because I needed the credits. But my major was in English literature. After I graduated, I quickly realized I was not going to be able to pay my rent as a painter. I also realized that the only marketable skill I had was the design bit that I had briefly studied. That, and I had been the editor of the arts section of our school newspaper. I went to school in Albany and the *Albany Student Press* had the largest circulation of any student newspaper in the country, so it was a pretty big deal. This is one of the reasons people went to school in Albany. I went just because my best friend did, and, at the time, it was the best state school that I could afford. So off I went to Albany, and got involved in the school newspaper. But, as it turned out, I didn't really like the editing part of it. What I *loved* was creating the design of the paper. I actually came out of college with this fantastic portfolio because it was a large format paper. I had a 12-page section that I did every week. I had these little magazines that I designed entirely by myself. I would give my friends articles to write and I wouldn't edit them. I'd publish them. There was this guy that was the campus clown. More like the campus soapbox guy. He was the political guy that would get up on his soapbox and talk about whatever political issue he thought. He was my favorite writer. I'd say, Hubert, write me an article about women's choice and he'd come back with 15 pages. I'd print the entire thing.

After I graduated and started looking for a job, I saw an ad in the *New York Times* for a magazine job at a publication called *Cable View*. The ad specifically stated "no visitors." Resumes only. I decided to go in person anyway figuring "what would they do, throw me out?" I figured I would just deliver the resume. They hired me that morning, on the spot, and I started right away. But they didn't really know what to make of me because I had this bizarre English/ Art degree. They put me in trafficking, and I ended up working in both the editorial and design departments concurrently. I did a little bit of design and a little bit of editing. It ended up being the perfect job. I could do everything I wanted to do and I loved it. I thought it was fantastic, but I couldn't live on the money. A year later I got offered a job at an advertising agency doing design, and I took it. It was real estate advertising, and all I did was design brochures for tasteless nondescript buildings. I knew the day that I quit *Cable View* I had made a terrible mistake because I cried for 48 hours. And it turned out that I did indeed make a mistake, as the work was dreadful, and I found that I hated doing work I didn't really believe in. I quit after a year and started working at *RockBill* magazine, again doing editing, writing, and design. Shortly thereafter, the creative director and I decided to start our own design firm. This was in 1987, and I had been working professionally for about four years at the time. Looking back on it, I don't know where I got the courage to start my own company! I think that I had more balls than I've probably ever had on any day of my life since or before. I had no idea how we were going to do it! We didn't have any money. We didn't have any clients. We didn't have really any contacts. But we did it anyway, and all of a sudden we had this business. All of a sudden we had a company, and then we had 20 people working for us. It was incredibly exciting. But ultimately, I didn't like the ethics of the company. And it was half mine! It's hard when you're working with one person because it's either you or them. Right now I have five partners. So if you disagree on something philosophically it becomes a round table. When you disagree with somebody philosophically and you only have one partner, it's an argument.

I realized that I was never going to be able to do something that I was really proud of in that particular business. Over the four years we were together, we made a lot of money. So, once again, I decided I don't want to do it anymore. At the time, I didn't know what I want to do in general, and I was very disillusioned. I had just turned 30. So, once again, I quit. I took a year off and I freelanced for Planned Parenthood and worked on their new identity. I did a brochure for a law firm and I traveled, and I thought about what I wanted to do. I decided that I wanted to work for the best design firm in the country (at the time), Frankfurt Balkind. Through a friend, I got an interview, and I showed Aubrey Balkind my portfolio. He said he'd hire me, but *not* as a designer; he didn't think my work was good enough. And this was all the work I had created in my entire career thus far! But I really wanted to work there, so I took the job he offered me: a job in marketing. About a year later, I got a call from a headhunter and he spoke to me about a job at a branding consultancy called The Schechter Group. I'd never done "formal" brand identity in my life. But it was incredibly compelling to me. When I gave Aubrey my notice, despite my not having been the world's greatest Marketing Director (and not having the smoothest of relationships with him) he looked me in the eye and told me that I was going to be very good in package design. He was right. For the first time in my life, I found my niche. I have been working in branding ever since and am blissfully happy all of the time.

*Joking!* I am actually very insecure and thus feel that I have to constantly prove myself every second of every day.

Currently, my day job is at Sterling Brands, where I am Chief Marketing Officer. I have been there for 20 years and helped grow the firm to the size it is now. I am also the Chair of the Masters in Branding Program at the School of Visual Arts and the Editor and Creative Director of *Print Magazine*. I also host the world's first design podcast, Design Matters with Debbie Millman.

***Do you have any techniques for presenting that you believe work particularly well?*** I take presentations very, very seriously. I prepare every second of every day—as every experience and every observation of the world contributes to how I present and what I present. I read a tremendous amount: newspapers, magazines, blogs, news sites, media sites, basically anything I can get my hands on or head around. That being said, I also do a substantial amount of research before I make a professional presentation: I investigate everything I can about a company and gather and read as much as possible. I believe that presentations are as much about communicating how much you understand a potential client as it is about communicating who you are and what you stand for.

I also believe in relentless preparation. Rudy Giuliani used to say that for every hour he spent in court, he would spend four hours preparing! I don't necessarily go to that extreme, but I do prepare quite a bit. I like to try and have as a goal that nothing unanticipated will happen (which is virtually impossible, but it's a goal!) and to ensure that, I find it is helpful to visualize every scenario and rehearse as much as you can. It is also helpful to anticipate the questions you might be asked, as well as the worst-case scenario (what will you do or say if your client hates everything???) in order to get you through anything that might happen. I also find it is beneficial to instill preparedness in others.

I also make sure that I have a sound strategic point of view and philosophy. Who we are as designers and what we believe in is as important as our ideas.

I consider my presentation style to be down to earth and accessible. I am not terribly funny, so I don't inject too much humor, but I do try to be warm and engaging. Good presentations are really about telling compelling, relevant, believable stories. I try to do this with as much authenticity and honesty as possible.

I don't get too nervous anymore. But I have been presenting for nearly 30 years. Occasionally I still do, when I speak in front of very large groups or when my technology fails. Once, at a HOW conference, in front of 1500 people, my projector would not sync with my laptop. That made me sweat. But if you are nervous, that doesn't give you the excuse to not prepare or not present! You must do it anyway. You can project confidence without necessarily feeling it! I recently read that Barbra Streisand's greatest talent isn't her singing or acting, but her ability to sing and act despite her massive stage fright. You just have to do it anyway. It is like going on a diet: You know you are going to be hungry, but you still don't eat as much. When presenting, you prepare yourself to be nervous, but you still have to get up and present. George Patton once said "All men are frightened, the more intelligent you are, the more frightened you are." So be frightened, but don't give yourself an out to not do what you know you need to do—and do well!

**How do you brainstorm? Are there any techniques you use or find par-
ticularly useful?** Idea generation is best encouraged with fun, safe, warm, and
encouraging environments. Dull focus-group room type facilities actually kill
ideas, rather than encourage them, so we want a lot of light, a lot of laughter,
and a lot of sharing to come up with new ideas.

Some additional tips that I have found useful when brainstorming are:

- Focus on ideas versus deliverables. Brainstorming should
  be about perceptions, not preferences.

- When brainstorming, make allowances for familiarity.
  People are generally more comfortable with what they
  know. And human beings, as a species, tend to be frightened of change.

- Brainstorming is an art, not a science. Try to investigate
  emotional connections and design sensibilities. Avoid an
  overdependence on thinking "it can't be done" or the
  "prove it can work" mentality.

- More is definitely merrier. Brainstorming is a time to
  develop scenarios, not solve problems. Come up with as
  many ideas as possible.

- Never say *no*. A brainstorm is the time for ideas not
  solutions.

**What advice would you give other creative directors or creatives who
aspire to make it to creative director and start their own company?**

- Be fearless when asking people for business.

- Find lots of clients. Because it's impossible to know which
  of them will be good.

- Work harder than anybody else that you know.

- Never give up if it is something that you really want.

- Don't lie about what you know and what you've done.

- Do not be afraid to want a lot.

- Things take a long time; practice patience.

- Avoid compulsively making things worse.

- Finish what you start.

- Often people start out by thinking about all the things
  that they can't do. Once you take that path, it's very hard
  to get off of it. Shoot high and shoot often.

# In a Nutshell

My work on this chapter has strengthened my belief that we can always depend on our fellow creatives for help. There is no need for animosity between creatives from different teams, agencies, studios, cities, or countries. Our goal should always be to do the best work possible to solve our client's marketing challenges. It's not about doing better than creatives in other agencies or studios. It's about doing better than we did yesterday. When you need help or advice with a project, don't be afraid to reach out to your contemporaries. Whether you're asking for advice or soliciting opinions, more often than not, you'll find that your fellow creative leaders are willing to lend a quick tip.

The creative professionals who answered my incredibly long list of questions answered them or interpreted them in their own ways. Each provided information on creative leadership, brainstorming, supervision, education, and team management from their perspective. As you can see, all of our journeys have been unique. From coast to coast and border to border, you will not find many creative career trajectories to be exactly the same. What you will find the same is a drive to be better; the drive that is leading or has led them to creative leadership. Now that you have benefitted from their wise words, as you work your way to the "promised land" of creative leadership, please be sure to pay it forward.

On your way, I only ask one thing: When that guy who gave the talk to the San Antonio chapter of AIGA titled "How not to suck as a Creative Director" reaches out to you and asks for your help with a book he is writing, please respond.

For my friends, both new and old, who responded to my call—Maria Claudia Camargo, Kim Arispe, Kevin Lane, Monica Ramirez Nadala, Lisette Sacks, Elizabeth Grace Saunders, Jessica Walsh, and Debbie Millman—thank you for your time and input. I am extremely grateful.

For those who did not respond and are now lamenting the tremendous opportunity that passed them by, all I can say is, "Respond to your e-mail!"

For those who avoided me because they may have seen me sitting in an unmarked car outside of their home with a sketchbook, rope, tape recorder, and camera, "Really?! Did you have to call the cops? I was just going to ask a couple questions!"

Who knows? Maybe I'll holla at you for the second edition of this book or maybe one of the other books that are in the works.

# The Final Nutshell

## Wait? Is it over already?

There you have it. My take on creative leadership—the good and the bad. Should you choose to embark on this career path, you will be faced with challenges from almost every direction. There will be times when you feel the world is a beautiful place full of sunshine and butterflies. But there will also be times when you'd love to take off on an extended coffee break and just give your clients the bird.

Sometimes the planets align; you get the promotions you seek, and everything works out perfectly. There may also be times when you're promoted and realize that the promotion was the worst thing that could have happened to you. There may even be times when you take a risk joining an "integrated" agency that promises the moon, and 90 days later you realize they really suck and you can't get out of there fast enough.

No matter what is going on remember this: You are a creative. You are being paid to be creative. You are not curing cancer. You are not developing life-saving immunizations for third-world countries. You are a creative leader or striving to be one. Don't allow yourself to get caught up in a negative mindset or get sucked into a negative work culture. Rise above it. Do what you do. Be creative. Sometimes we get hung up on what PMS color a logo should be or why a client didn't like our choice of typeface. Don't sweat that. You can only lead your

© Eleazar Hernández 2017

E. Hernández, *Leading Creative Teams*, DOI 10.1007/978-1-4842-2056-6_14

client so far. In the end, it's their product, their money, their decision. Discuss your decisions as clearly as you can and then move on. Lead your team. Lead them well. Do the job to the best of your ability; that's all you can do.

# You Can Do It

There will be long nights filled with self-doubt and diminishing confidence. You will wonder if you'll be able to come up with an idea *this* time? The pressure to come up with good ideas will never decrease. Know that you are not alone. Depend on your team. Utilize their skills and help build them into a cohesive unit. Support them and they will support you.

That's the nature of the creative industry. Rise or fall, if you are striving to be a great creative leader, you will be a better person for at least trying. Know that these can be the best and most exciting years of your working life. Revel in it.

Over the course of my career, I have found that there are several things that I have become increasingly focused on: creative leadership, brainstorming, sketching, the creative process, and running nude in a field of daisies. Ha! Just checking to see if you were still paying attention.

My hope is that by writing this book, I have illuminated some of the highpoints and challenges you will experience on your way to creative leadership along with providing you with some solid tools to help you cope with these challenges.

Do I have all the answers? Nope, but I do have 20 years of experience from which to draw. Within those 20 years I have experienced great successes, but I have also dealt with my fair share of B.S. as well as witnessed the mistakes of others. In the end, I feel every opportunity provided a lesson to be learned. Did I learn from all of them? Sort of. Honestly, I still deal with certain struggles. For example, I still have a hard time dealing with duplicitous, conniving individuals who spend their work hours causing strife and conflict.

While I did write this book, I do not believe it is the end-all source of creative leadership wisdom. Do I have opinions, insights, stories, and jokes? Yup, yup. You know it. I hope that you've found everything both entertaining and enlightening.

# Talk to Me

For those of you who found this book to be helpful, I would love to hear from you. If you found the information inspiring and thought to yourself, "Uh huh, that's right." Holla at me, I'd love to hear how you utilized the information. Your wins, losses, ups, and downs. Better yet, if while you read this book you sprung to your feet in a crowded room and exclaimed, "Amen, amen, AMEN HALLELUYAH!" Oh, yeah... we should chat. You can contact me at comments@elihernandez.com.

Now for those of you who thought this book fell short of your expectations and believe I didn't touch any of the important topics you wanted or expected me to, send your thoughtful comments and opinions my way; I'd be happy to consider them for inclusion in the next book. Please be gentle with any negative criticisms.

# It's Up to You

Now that you've reached the end of the book, go back and make your way through it again. Write notes in the margins. Highlight to your heart's content. Try to integrate some or all of the tips into your work flow and creative processes. Go for it. At the very least, you will add to your skillset. No matter what stage of your career you are in, you should always strive to be better. You can do it!

Be more than a designer!

Be more than an art director!

Be more than a web designer or developer!

Be more than a copywriter!

Strive to be a great creative leader!

Now go forth. Lead your team. Be fruitful and multiple...

#wepa

# Index

© Eleazar Hernandez 2017
E. Hernandez, *Leading Creative Teams*, DOI 10.1007/978-1-4842-2056-6

# Get the eBook for only $5!

Why limit yourself?

Now you can take the weightless companion with you wherever you go and access your content on your PC, phone, tablet, or reader.

Since you've purchased this print book, we're happy to offer you the eBook in all 3 formats for just $5.

Convenient and fully searchable, the PDF version enables you to easily find and copy code—or perform examples by quickly toggling between instructions and applications. The MOBI format is ideal for your Kindle, while the ePUB can be utilized on a variety of mobile devices.

To learn more, go to www.apress.com/companion or contact support@apress.com.

Printed in the United States
By Bookmasters